Get Off The Grass

Wayne Chaffey

Published by Wayne "Chuck" Chaffey, 2024.

While every precaution has been taken in the preparation of this book, the publisher assumes no responsibility for errors or omissions, or for damages resulting from the use of the information contained herein.

GET OFF THE GRASS

First edition. April 30, 2024.

Copyright © 2024 Wayne Chaffey.

ISBN: 979-8215464557

Written by Wayne Chaffey.

Preface

HI, MY NAME IS WAYNE Chaffey and I served in the Royal Australian Air Force (RAAF) from 1980 – 2011, with some breaks in between, my job title being: Ground Support Equipment Fitter (GSEFITT).

This is my story about my 24 years of working in the Defence Force.

I talk about my ups and downs associated with this career choice, and also give an insight of how life can be when compared to any other career path, and not necessarily what many perceive as too disciplined and restrictive.

Although only a Corporal when I was discharged, I too have a story to tell, which many will find relatable with more in the way of ground roots situations, applicable to the ordinary ranks.

I would like to thank my wife, Huey Yi, for pre-editing my book and heading me in the right direction, as this is my first book I needed inspiration at times, and she was able to give it to me when needed.

Huge thanks also go to 2 of my dear friends who also took the time to go through the book, offering their suggestions, many of which I incorporated with appreciation.

These 2 being: Leonard Jeyam and Karen Lee.

Table of contents

GET OFF THE GRASS

An autobiography of my 24 years of service with the Royal Australian Air Force (RAAF)

Chapter 1
Recruits

Let me set the scene:

MY STORY BEGINS IN 1980 when I was working for Stilwell Ford, a motor vehicle dealership in Medindie.

Medindie is a suburb not too far from the Central Business District (CBD) of Adelaide; I was employed as a Motor Mechanic here.

Around this time, business was slowing down for mechanical workshops in the Adelaide area, some were downsizing and some were closing down, a sign of the times I guess.

Although Stilwell Ford wasn't particularly in this position, having a young family consisting of a wife and our 1-year-old daughter Kristy, I was concerned about job security. Thus I thought of joining the Australian Army as this would ease the stress related to uncertainty and the possibility of being out of work.

Thereafter, I organised an appointment and off I went to the recruiting office. I was feeling a little nervous at this time as I have never been in this situation before and didn't really know what to expect.

I rolled up finding a group of guys also waiting to apply, many younger than me. I remember thinking to myself, how many would be accepted today?

Everything as you would imagine was done very efficiently and in an orderly way; there were many different forms to fill out at the start and then medical, aptitude and psychological evaluations carried out as the day went on.

Upon passing all the tests, I was advised my application would be deferred for 6 months, due to the fact that basic training was carried out in Wagga Wagga in New South Wales and I would be away from my family for 3 months. This was also to give me time to decide if that would be acceptable.

While waiting for this time to go by, I was introduced by a friend of my wife's to a couple of Air Force instructors.

Air Force! This was completely out of left field, not even thinking about the Air Force as the Army was marketed so well, not to mention Air Force basic training was carried out only 30 minutes away from where I was living at the time.

The instructors gave me the rundown of what the Air Force had over the Army as far as training, life style and conditions. They informed me that the Air force is far less combat-focused than the Army, where the primary objective is a supporting role revolving around the Aircraft. Recruit training is done just out of Adelaide and their housing is far better than that of the Army. This blew me away and totally convinced me that I should join. I went into the recruiting centre once more and applied to join the RAAF. I breezed through the application process.

They were in need of Motor Mechanics at the time and the bonus for them was I wouldn't have to be trained; I joined as a qualified tradesman known in the defence force as a Direct Entry.

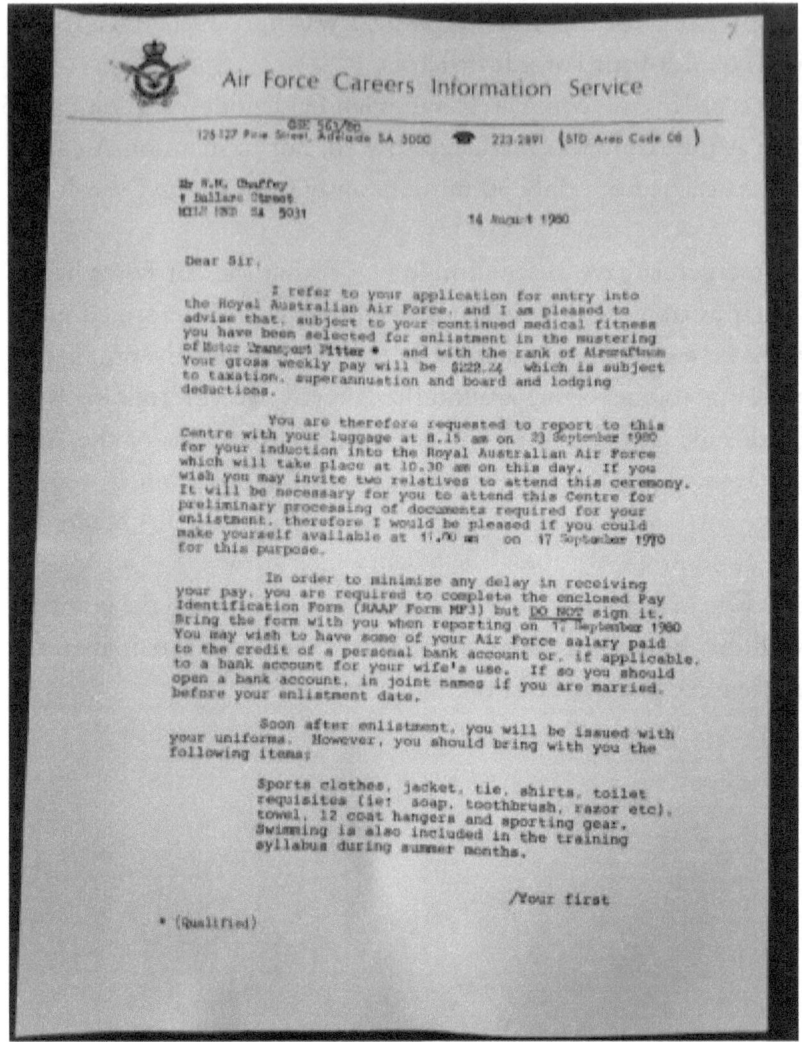

My original acceptance letter

Soon after all my security checks had been carried out, I was off to No. 1 Recruit Training Unit (1RTU) RAAF Base Edinburgh, being in the suburb of Edinburgh approximately a 20-30 minute drive North of where I was living at the time. I should say at this point that this is a male-only training facility. Female recruits at this time were being trained at RAAF Laverton (near Melbourne), if memory serves me correctly.

This was an exciting time for me, a new lease of life in a career nothing like what I had or would encounter in a civilian setting.

I couldn't wait to start; I was one of the oldest in my group at 23 years old, the rest maybe around 18 *years of age*.

The expectation of what I was going to encounter while on course was a little vague to say the least, other than what I was informed of at the recruiting centre and something that stayed in my mind was "expect a huge culture shock"! I'm not sure who told me that, someone who had experienced I expect. This is going back a while and some of what happened is a little faded to say the least, but I will try my best to recollect my experiences.

My wife drove me to the base where I would be staying for the next 4 weeks out of the 12 that the course ran for. After that I would be able to apply to live off base as my house was within the allowed distance and commute daily. The other guys (recruits) were from all over Australia. I was the only local.

This is where we met our instructor, a Corporal Air Force Defence Guard (ADG) and were formed into ranks of some sort. This was known as a Flight which consisted of 24 men (from memory), 3 ranks of 8. Orders were being barked left, right and centre, we didn't know what hit us. It was a comedy of errors especially when an order to turn was given, knowing your left from your right was completely forgotten for most, ending up with some guys facing each other throughout the flight and to laugh was not on, which was usually met with an instructor yelling at you asking what you found so funny.

As far as I can remember we arrived approximately 1 week prior to the course commencing and were put on "Pool duty" where we were used as a labour force in different parts of the base. I was sent to Ground Equipment Maintenance Section (GEMS), 492 SQN, at the "sharp" (business) end of the base, while waiting for the course to commence, where I experienced some of the vehicles and equipment that I would be working on once through rookies. I really enjoyed working with the guys that would be my colleagues a little further down the track.

At some stage we were given our service numbers verbally and expected to remember them. Mine was A410384; "A" denoted Air Force, the first number, 4 in my case, denoted what state you enlisted in, that was a great shemozzle for whenever you were called, your service number was used. I guess to ram it into your skull as it were; the first rank we received was that of Air Craftsman Recruit (ACR).

Before anything else though, we had to organise our accommodation being in "Siberia", a part of the base out on its own that hadn't been used for a while and was in need of a good going over.

The standard of cleanliness during recruit training "Rookies" was very high as you could imagine so it was a huge job to get this block to the standard needed.

The floors were Lino tiles which had to be scrubbed and polished with an industrial electric polisher; this brute of a thing took some time getting to learn as it had a mind of its own and would take you anywhere it wanted until you reined it in. Needless to say the ablutions had to be spotless to a fault, even the urinal had to be scrubbed and polished by hand; we were only issued working dress at this time. As recruits we were only able to bring a limited amount of civilian clothing, all military clothing was supplied, including underwear, as well as toiletries.

Start of Course

The next chains of events are not necessarily in order, due to the intensity of the course and memory constraints.

This was 23SEP80 and I was on the No. 1578 Recruit Training Course.

There was one recruit designated as "Course Horse" whose responsibility was to make sure everyone was ready for whatever was about to commence be it a lesson, physical training or meals and get us formed up and march to wherever we had to be. Thankfully the recruit who was given the task was ex-Army and had a good idea of what to do.

Every morning we would form into a flight outside our accommodation and "March" (we would march everywhere, no walking allowed) to the "Mess" (dining room) and line up for breakfast, although for the first few days "March" was a very loose term. The newest courses were at the back of the line-up, with about 10 or so courses ahead of us, it took a while to actually get to the mess, having to wait for available seats.

We would march back to our accommodation singly or in small groups once finished, and get ready for the first lesson of the day. Everything was on a tight schedule, sometimes meals would have to be gulped down to make it back on time and this was very frustrating for me as I was a slower eater than most.

From memory, one of the first things we did was to march down to the clothing store or "L Group" to be issued the remainder of our kit. This was quite extensive being divided into 2 main groups, "Public" and "Service issue". Public clothing was clothing that could be exchanged if damaged or worn out, such as working uniform, boots, etc., and was never owned by the member and would be handed back in on discharge, where Service issue were items such as Dress uniform, service shoes, tie, hat, etc., and was owned by the member and not exchangeable.

Once we had all our kit we were shown how to iron, fold and where to put it all in our wardrobe as everything had its correct place. This seemed to be overkill to me, but all part of the discipline that was hammered down our throats. All the drawers in our wardrobe had to be lined with fresh newspaper every week with the date situated in a certain position to be easily seen and to prove we had changed it. All issued items such as our jocks, socks, and handkerchiefs had to be folded correctly and had their places, along with toiletries such as shaver (the type that had a single, double sided blade which no one used), shaving brush, comb, toothbrush, etc. This was so frustrating, as it all took time of which we didn't really have enough of, but if done incorrectly everything would be tossed out by the instructors and have to be redone again.

The next job was how to prepare our boots; these were hard-soled, lace-up, mid-calf army boots which had to be slightly modified to become our parade boots. The toe cap was to be rubbed back with sand paper to remove all imperfections and the pattern pressed into the leather, to enable a build-up of boot polish to become smooth and highly polished and stand out from the remainder of the boot. We were even shown how to "spit polish", yes you guessed it, using spit, my god how disgusting, but it does work.

We also had to learn how to make our beds to rookie specifications, the sheets were to be tucked under using hospital corners and the top sheet was turned down a particular distance without any wrinkles (most guys ironed that section), the counterpane had a large Air Force crest on it and that had to be lined up as specified, the blankets had a particular striped design on them and would be folded in a particular way, so as to line up the stripes and would be placed at the end of the bed.

Normally two guys would help each other make their beds as some of this would take too long to do alone, and this was done every day. We would have 'stand by bed' inspections at the whim of the instructor, who would have something different to pick on every time; this would include every aspect of our layout including ourselves. At times we would come back to our barracks to find the place turned upside down, where some other instructors have come in and pulled everything out of our drawers, pulled our beds apart or tipped over, just to give us more to do that evening.

Every morning before the first lesson we would be inspected for dress and bearing, which included clean and correctly ironed uniform, haircut, clean shaved, polished brass on our belts, cleanliness and spit polish of our boots. Now I knew what was meant by "culture shock".

The pressure was put on us from day one with no let up, we could be up until 11.00 pm some nights getting ready for the next day, especially on "panic night", where we had to have the whole block spotless for inspection the next day, and from memory this was usually on Sunday nights.

The main emphasis was on teamwork, supporting each other was the only way to get through the course without too many hitches. This was generally learnt the hard way, if one rookie stuffed up, the whole course would pay the price; this was particularly prevalent during drill sessions. All drills were done by numbers (1 being the action and 2,3 being the pause before the next action) and at a particular cadence and for some this was a real challenge, knowing your left from your right was also a problem at times, so we would keep doing the same drill movement until all got it right. Sometimes that could take us well past knock off time and even encroach into meal times. Of course there would be some on the spot "punishment" such as "get down and give me 10" (push ups), if a troop insisted on getting something wrong continually.

This could make it hard for the person or persons having trouble and would put undue pressure on them to get it right, it wouldn't be unusual for a little one on one coaching to be carried out between rookies after hours, as well as some counselling (if you catch my drift).

We were constantly being appraised and there was always the thought of being back coursed if we didn't come up to expectations and no one wanted to be a rookie for any longer than they had to be. For some, this could become too much and some talked of quitting, but would be talked down by their peers and made to realise that it was only this intense for 12 weeks and we just had to handle it, but we may have lost one or two through the course due to this.

Some of the training methods used were a little belittling at times, for example "eyes ahead" was the norm when marching or at attention, yet some were easily distracted and would be caught looking at the instructor as he walked up and down giving instructions and would be met with something like **"are you in love with me"** or **"can't you keep your eyes off me"** yelled at him and the recruit would have to answer loud enough for everyone to hear and of course "get down and give me 10".

Another distraction was where the instructor carried a little red book and would put it down somewhere in front of the flight, where he would catch someone looking at it, which was met with **"do you love that little red book? then go over and tell it"**, the recruit would have to come to attention and march over to the book and say loudly **"I love you little red book"**, repeating the sentence if it wasn't loud enough and march back. You can imagine the shame. Needless to say this would only happen once.

Every now and then a stressed out recruit would answer the instructor as "Sir" as in "Yes Sir" and that would be replied with "Don't call me sir, I work for a living", normally in a humorous way. As we progressed we all grew more confident, knowing more or less what to expect which took the edge off and made everything more tolerable.

One of the nicest guys you would ever want to meet was on my course and he had a particular problem with underarm odour. If you were marching behind him it was hard to cope with and we all noticed it, so we got together to discuss how to tell him without offending him.

I came up with the idea to tell him that using under arm deodorant would help with the chaffing under the arms, caused by the amount of marching we did and presented him with a roll on deodorant, he took it on board and was very thankful and so were we.

A lot of time was focused on drill, drill and more drill, so much to learn as it had to become second nature; attention, stand at ease, open order march, right dress, salute to the right, salute to the left, incline march, change step, halt, quick march, move to the right in three's right turn, to name a few and this is before we were doing rifle drill which would offer a whole lot more. I found this confusing at times, but it all came together eventually.

This is an example of our uniform although the pullovers are for a cooler time of the year

We would also undergo quite a lot of physical training, I remember the first exercise we were given were leg raises. Most of us were new to this particular exercise. This took place outside on the bitumen parade ground, lying on our backs we would have to bring our legs to 90 degrees and hold for what seemed like forever (probably 8 minutes or so), then bring them to approximately 30cm forward of that position and hold again for 5 minutes, then just off the ground for another 5 minutes.

There were lots of groans and moans coming from everywhere, with no rest, back up to 90 degrees and so on. This was a rude awakening for everyone and a sign of things to come.

There were set PT uniforms we had to wear and we were inspected every session, mainly looking for cleanliness and properly ironed clothing. The laces of our sport shoes had to be washed after every lesson as they would be grass and mud stained. If they couldn't be cleaned in that fashion we would have to use sand shoe whitener, the same went for the shoes, the shoe laces would also have to be flat without any twists, all shoe and boot laces were subject to this, we were issued Dunlop Volleys.

Funny thing I remember was whenever we were formed up in a flight while at a PT session, and were given the order to turn while stationary, instead of doing a normal turn we would have to do a sort of bunny hop turn and when marching it would always be at double time.

Part of our training included an obstacle course that we had to get through, one of the obstacles was a high wall, the technique we used to get over this wall was where one guy would cup his hands down in front of him, about 40cm off the ground, to enable a foot hold and the person scaling the wall would put his foot into his hands and push up and grab the edge of the wall. When it came time for me to do this, I guess I was a little exuberant and managed to knee the other guy in the chin and almost knock him out, for some reason he wasn't too happy with me after that, that was a little embarrassing, but he should have been watching more closely.

We were taught other skills as well as our military training, such as firefighting using a 75mm fire hose with full mains pressure, this would lift some of the smaller guys off the ground with the pressure, that was funny to watch, as well as recognising the different types of fire extinguishers available and how to use them, this among other firefighting implements and their uses. I think we also learnt some basic first aid that could be used in our work environment, as well as day to day use.

I think one of the most important skill sets we learnt was teamwork, communication and how to get along with other people. I remember one of the young recruits stating at the very beginning that, "nobody is going to tell me what to do". Well that was going to change fairly quickly and many could also be quite rude at times, but due to the training methods adopted as well as living in close proximity, everybody emerged from the course a better person.

The 4-week mark was up and I was able to live off base, back home with my family, that was a great feeling. Unfortunately, there were a few cons to go along with the pros. I still had to maintain my living area the same as if I was still on base and share the same duties, I had to get to base early, as from memory I was to change into uniform once there.

Shortly after I was living off base, I had my house up for sale and had to get home quickly that evening as the agent had a buyer coming around.

I drove through the base a bit quicker than 40kph (the speed limit on base) that day, and once off the base took off like a mad man.

Well I was to report to the Sergeant in charge of 1RTU the next morning and was informed I was banned from driving on base, as the Commanding Officer of 1RTU spotted me going a little too quickly on base and followed me and when I turned out of the base he couldn't catch me. Apparently he got up to 110 kph, I was told the road outside the base is in the jurisdiction of RAAF Edinburgh and is a 60kph zone.

Do you think that pissed me off? From then on I had to park in the visitor's car park at the front of the base and walk briskly 15 mins or so to the accommodation block, no big deal I suppose. It just made things that little bit harder. The thing with that was, short cuts across any grassed area or the parade ground were definitely forbidden and if seen, even from a distance, "**Get off the grass** or **parade ground**" would be yelled and that scared the life out of you, you just didn't want that. As time marched on so did we, the end of course was getting closer and we were getting further up the meal line.

Eventually we were issued our rifles and started to learn how they worked, along with a whole lot of new drill to go with it, the weapons we used were SLRs (Self Loading Rifle), reasonably heavy and something totally new to us, the rifles employed what is known as open sights, nothing optical like some of today's weapons. This opened up an opportunity for more mistakes to be made when learning the drill associated with rifles, and more punishment's to boot, I thought OMG here we go. One of these punishments was marching double time around the parade ground with the rifle held over your head with arms stretched, for as long as the instructor saw fit, another was holding the rifle directly out in front of you, again to the instructors discretion. Of course the discipline associated with weapon handling had to be at a high level; after all it is a killing implement.

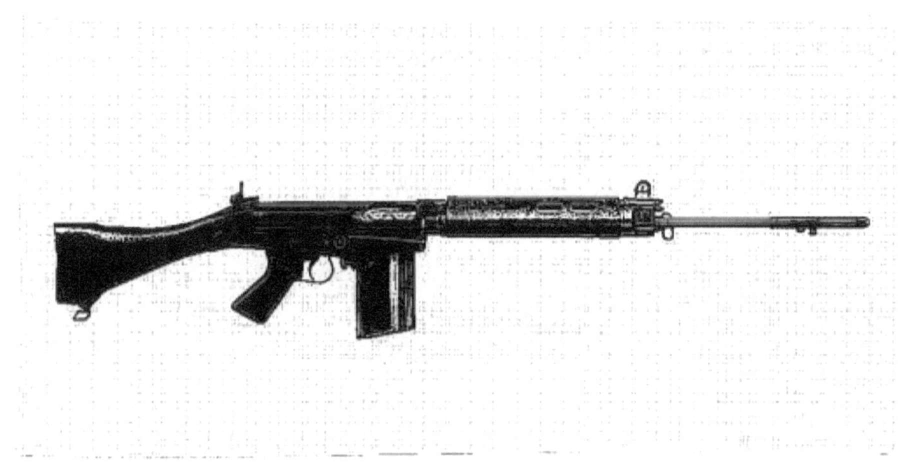

L1A1 Self Loading Rifle (SLR)

Once we were proficient enough with the SLR we would be tested before we could get on the firing range. The rifle also had to be completely stripped down to its many parts and laid down in order and reassembled in the correct sequence, I think one or two mistakes were allowed other than safety issues, where there were no mistakes permitted.

Our first shoot was carried out at the 25 metre range on base. We had previously learnt the 4 positions we would be firing from being: prone (lying), sitting, kneeling and standing, before we were allowed on the range. We were to load the magazines that we would be using, in a separate area away from the range lanes and they would be issued to us once we were in position ready to fire, starting from the prone position, this is where our previous training would come to fruition.

We used appropriate hearing protection being ear muffs and would be given the order to put them on; the next order would be "With a magazine of 20 rounds Load", that's when the heart starts to race.

The next order was "Action" where the weapon was cocked still with the safety on, then "Instant" the safety was taken off, then "Target at immediate front, 5 sighting rounds, Fire", remembering all we had previously been taught about breathing, sighting, shouldering the weapon, kicked in. We were warned about the recoil of the weapon and how the front sight can cut above your eye if held too close, of which I experienced at one time, and a kick there was, it was very exciting getting the first rounds off and landing on the target. With instructors closely watching everyone, there was a feeling of reassurance, as some recruits were more hazardous than others, waving their rifles around rather than keeping them pointing down range. It was a great experience. Once the shoot was finished we would gather all the brass casings, ejected all over the range in our bush hats and put them in empty ammo containers.

Then there was the arduous task of cleaning our rifles to the highest standard.

Hard carbon residue would be on all the parts subject to the high temperatures created by the explosion of the round when fired, and would need to be cleaned before the next firing of the weapon could occur, this was to be accomplished with the use of a nylon brush similar to a tooth brush only harder, purposely made cloth, gun oil and a "pull through". The "pull through" was used for cleaning inside the barrel and consisted of a rope with a weight attached to one end, and a loop approximately one metre further down at the other end.

A piece of cleaning cloth, which was measured by lines printed on the cloth, called a "4x2" due to the dimensions of the cloth, was positioned halfway through the loop along with a few drops of gun oil. The weighted end of the rope would be fed down the barrel until the cloth started to enter, and then with one action the rope would be pulled through the barrel cleaning as it went.

Now on the odd occasion because the person carrying out the pull through, couldn't complete the action in one movement or the cloth was too big, it could get stuck in the barrel rendering the rifle useless, and it would have to be taken by the person cleaning it to the "gunnies" or armourers to be removed, remembering this is a rookie taking his rifle to a qualified armourer, imagine the rhetoric involved, hence a nervousness when carrying out a pull through.

When we had the skills required for a qualifying shoot, we were taken to the local 300 metre range at Murray Bridge which is about 1 hr east of Adelaide.

At one stage we were shown how to shoot from the hip, where I had an incident where the rifle "broke" into two while I was firing (the rifle has a catch on the side to lock it together, this is where it is hinged to open and allow access to the barrel and working parts for cleaning etc., and to all intent and purposes when it is open it looks as if its broken in two: refer picture, I'm not sure how it happened, maybe it wasn't properly closed in the first place, nothing was said so I expect it wasn't noticed by my instructors before I remedied it, but still it was panic stations for me.

SLR stripped

So time marched on and It was the end of Rookies finally, and I hadn't been caught out for anything uniform related throughout the course, (meaning I wasn't put in the position where I had to front up to the instructors at lunch time, or at the end of the day, in inspection order because my uniform was not up to expectations on morning parade, so the instructors decided I had to report to them on the last day purely for that reason.

So I reported at lunch time to be inspected, but no one was there, I waited for a while but still no one, sneaky buggers, got me on that one. I guess they just wanted to piss me off and succeeded.

Generally at the end of course there is a march out parade carried out, where invited family and guests would witness the formality of a march by in full uniform, but due to the heat at that time of year; 45 degrees Celsius, where soles of shoes were melting, and people fainting, my course was denied that and a smaller celebration was carried out indoors.

Chapter 2

My first posting – RAAF Amberley

NOW THAT ROOKIES WAS over it was time to organise removals from where my family and I were living at the time to my new location. I had sold my house in Adelaide, the next thing to do was to inform the removal company when to come and pack everything.

We had already carried out an inventory, that was a huge stress as everything had to be itemised down to every knife, fork and spoon, a huge undertaking, but the trade-off was that the removalists packed everything.

At the beginning of rookies we nominated 3 preferences for posting upon completion of recruit/trade training, the Air Force would do their best to post you to a base amongst those, this was of course dependent on manning requirements at the time, I think I was the only one who was a direct entry and was to proceed directly to a base, the other guys where off to Wagga Wagga NSW for trade training.

I had nominated Queensland, Northern Territory and Western Australia.

I was lucky enough to be posted to No.3 Aircraft Depot (3AD), RAAF Base Amberley, which is situated approximately 1 hour west of Brisbane in Queensland.

This is the largest base in Australia, which at the time comprised many different aircraft squadrons including 1 & 6 Sqn with F111 fighter/bomber's (Pig being their nick name), 12 Sqn with Chinook twin rotor helicopters (Chook), 9 Sqn with Iroquois helicopters, (Huey).

An F111 flying over RAAF Amberley

3AD was a major refurbishment unit for aircraft as well as vehicles, the section I worked for was known as Ground Equipment Maintenance Section (GEMS). There were all the allied trades needed to support the vehicle refurbishment process under the same roof, such as; painters, upholsters, motor body builders and of course motor mechanics known as Motor Transport Fitters (MTFITT). Being a direct entry my rank was Leading Air Craftsman (LAC) as soon as I finished rookies, which was accompanied with the applicable pay rise. All positions in the RAAF are known as Mustering's and referred to by their acronyms, mine being MTFITT (Gr1), it took a while to get to know all the different Mustering's.

We could choose whether we wanted to drive or fly and have our vehicle/s transported to our new base, my the decision was to drive, a lot more convenient. We would be given a certain amount of days along with sufficient funds to cover fuel, accommodation and food for the trip, once at our destination we would be put up in a Motel or self-contained unit for approximately 2 weeks while we found a RAAF married quarter, and waited for our possessions to arrive, we would receive allowances to cover food while we were waiting.

Because of the time of year that we arrived, being Christmas, the base was basically shutdown due to most personal being on leave, with just a skeleton crew manning it; therefore I was unable to start work until the base was in full swing again. I was able to enquire whether we could stay in a motel somewhere else and the answer was yes, nice, with Surfer's paradise only 1.5 hrs away I was able to book us into a motel down there for a week. This was very convenient as my parents were holidaying down there also, a free holiday on the RAAF, cool.

Holiday over, now was the time to learn about the real Air Force. On my first day I was to report to the orderly room to sign in and find out where my unit was.

3AD's Headquarters building was huge and carpark to suit, the building wasn't hard to find, but a suitable carpark took a while. I had a map to help me find things, but still a little daunting.

I was given a clearance form which is basically all the relevant departments/ sections on the base that I need to sign into so they know I'm here, this would need to be completed within a week or so and then handed back to the orderly room completed.

This was a great way to get to know where some of the important sections of the base are, and meet some of the key personnel involved with the running of the base, including the CO.

The first stop was my own section and to meet my boss, I can't remember if the first point of contact was with the Officer in Charge (OIC) "Sir" or my Warrant Officer (Woff) also "Sir", either way I was introduced to all my chain of command that was in the office at that time, including the Flight Sergeant (FSGT) known as "Flight", my Sergeant (SGT) "Serge" and then my Corporal (CPL) Don, being his first name, who introduced me to all the troops in the workshop, and also gave me a guided tour of the base and all the places I would have to visit for my clearances.

It was so different to rookies as far as how relaxed everyone was, of course the discipline was still there, but at a more realistic level, no more marching everywhere, but still coming to attention and saluting officers when approaching them.

Over the next week I started getting to know the machinery and equipment I would be working with, as well as completing my clearances. Don more or less took me under his wing as I worked with him most of the time, while I was getting to know the setup and how things worked. In the mean time we selected a married quarter from 5 or so offered to us and organised our belongings to be taken there.

The RAAF had their own area for married quarters comprising 100s of houses, expressly for RAAF personnel in the small town of Leichardt only a small distance from the base. The house was on a road that divided the public housing department sector from the RAAF sector. This didn't present any problems for us, but unfortunately there seemed to be some that saw RAAF personnel as getting a better deal than them, due to having a good job and earning a good wage. Angry confrontations were not unusual at times; luckily we had peaceful neighbours over the road from us and once it was known I was a motor mechanic, I was called upon to carry out the occasional repair.

Our house was a high set "Queenslander" style place, and I was able to set up a reasonable workshop underneath, rebuilt a few engines and rebuilt my mini. One of the engine rebuilds I carried out was for a RAAF Doctor, who wanted to help, this came as a surprise as I wouldn't have thought someone in his position would like getting their hands dirty. Another one was for a civilian. This was an old Ford V8, very challenging because of its size and weight. After completing it he came around with a trailer and "helped" me winch it off the bench, I secured it at one end and he the other, at least that's what he confirmed he had done, instead of it coming up off the bench level it actually rolled off the bench and landed on the ground upside down, it looked ok other than a small dent on one of the rocker covers, he said no problems I'll fix that when I get it home.

He got it home and put it in his car, it started and ran, but there wasn't any oil pressure so he revved it up thinking that would help, but no luck. (This is really bad for an engine especially a new one). Only then did he call me, I was shocked to hear what he had done (revving the engine), I tried to think what could have happened, when I remembered a shaft the size and shape of a pencil that went from the bottom of the distributor to turn the oil pump, this must have dislodged when the engine fell on its head. When I got to his place sure enough this was the problem, now how to get at it to refit it as it was deep in the engine, he came up with the idea to use his arc welder to attach a welding rod to the shaft enabling it to be removed.

This was comical to watch as this procedure creates huge sparks and at that precise moment it ignited the oil around the area and shot flames out of the distributor access hole, shocking the hell out of both of us especially him, needless to say this didn't work. Then I thought of using a thin magnet used for retrieving nuts and bolts from hard to get places. This did the job. What a drama.

While at Amberley, I rebuilt a Morris Mini Deluxe, giving it a relatively new interior and a complete colour change, and of course a reworked engine that made nearly twice as much power as the original, this is what I loved doing - modifying cars and motorbikes to look and go better than original, I had done this all my life and still do.

My 1964 Mini Deluxe before rebuild

1964 Mini Deluxe after rebuild

One thing I remember about the house was the orientation of the windows; they opened to the left and any sound or voice coming from that direction would bounce into the room clear as day, and one would swear there was a person in the room. That took quite a while to get used to and yes another thing I remember was the floor boards, which were uncovered and had a small gap between them to allow air flow in the warmer months. They also allowed cockroaches to come into the house; I'm talking 2 inches long, generally during the night when there was minimal movement, you could come into the kitchen to get a drink and the floor would move, open the draw to get a spoon and they would crawl up your arm, we would get the RAAF Hygiene department, aka "Rat catchers" in to treat under the house and they would go for a while, but they fly in from all over especially from banana trees which were in many backyards throughout the married quarters. It was gross, but unfortunately not a lot could be done.

Our house was in direct line with the flight path that the F111 fighter's took when returning to base at the end of the day and night, which just happened to be around the same time our favourite "soap" was on TV, not only were they noisy, but the signal would scramble and do strange things to the visuals, they would also return from their night sorties around 11.00 pm and have their landing lights on lighting up the whole house this was a little disturbing, but the trade-off was they were so low and looked great, the noise the jet engines made was exciting, something I never got tired of.

During the summer we would encounter flooding rains; making it difficult to get into work at times. There were different routes to take, one lead to the front gate and one leading to the back gate of which the majority of us would take, as the roads coming from the married quarters would join up with it. I remember one road would traverse a bridge where the river could rapidly rise and cover it cutting off access to the front gate. We could be cut off from the base completely for hours or days, and if we made it to work it could be the same situation on the return home, but normally we would be sent home early if needed before more rain came.

In April 1981 celebrations for The Diamond Jubilee of the RAAF were topped with an air show at RAAF Amberley, where the majority of the base was open to the public with static displays and fantastic air displays. I remember camera crews in Iroquois helicopters hovering for 2.5 hours, broadcasting live for the ABC. We had displays of some of the equipment we used and maintained, and would be in uniform manning them ready to answer questions. I had only been in the RAAF for a short time and this was a real eye opener, to see everything the RAAF had to offer in the air over my base, doing incredible things.

Ok back to work, one of the main roles my section played was refurbishing Truck Fire General Purpose (TFGP) domestic fire trucks, where they were stripped down to the chassis and every component was rebuilt or replaced, including a complete engine overhaul giving the truck a "new life". During the refurbishment the engine was completely reconditioned, where we would set it up on a piece of equipment called an engine dynamometer. Here we could run the engine mimicking driving conditions for 8 hours, a similar process to running in a new car; this would allow all the new components of the engine to "bed in". Throughout this process we would also run the engine at maximum power for short bursts, to ensure it was stable enough to perform properly at full throttle, during these bursts the exhaust manifolds would get so hot they would glow orange and become transparent.

All mechanised equipment as well as some stationary equipment such as generators etc. at that time were given a "life", where every hour that was used for maintenance was accounted for, and when a predetermined number of hours were reached the vehicle would be refurbished and given a new "life". This would happen a certain amount of times before it was decommissioned, hence there were some old pieces of equipment still around.

We also maintained many other types of equipment e.g. refuelling tankers, aircraft loading platforms. One of which was a scissor lift with a faulty carburettor, the new part was being sourced from Germany and it took over a year for it to be delivered as it was particular to this piece of equipment, and was very hard to find.

We would come across this sort of thing from time to time, due to some of the ill-informed sourcing deals done in the Defence force.

The thing I found the hardest to come to grips with was slowing down to the pace "required" in the workshop, coming from an environment where I had to put 110% in every day, literally running around the workshop to get things done (by the way I loved the pressure, being the only way I knew at that time). At one stage someone said to me "you have to slow down or we'll be painting rocks", this is what actually happened when the months' work schedule was finished, to give us something to do we would paint the rocks that marked out certain areas around our section, therefore we had to pace the workload throughout the month.

Every year we would be evaluated for performance, service attitude etc. and the scores from the evaluation would be used to position each individual for promotion prospects and the main criticism I would receive for the first 2 years was to, you guessed it, slow down.

This was primarily down to manning requirements where our numbers could be reduced, due to it being seen that we didn't have enough work to sustain the workforce that we had and that we were overstaffed, in essence that wasn't the case as in the busy months we would be working overtime to get everything out.

To fill the day, the norm was to stop and have a chat with someone on your way to the tool store for example, out of the sight of the bosses of course, or to visit someone working in a different area of the base; I also had to bring my walking pace down to a stroll, I found this very pleasing once I got used to it.

Some guys that weren't particularly proficient at their job, would walk around with clip boards under their arms, looking more organised than some others, and in the eyes of the bosses this was a good thing, little did they know this was just for appearance sake. These guys would be more likely to be promoted sooner than others.

On one occasion after completing the refurbishment of a TFGP fire truck, Don and myself took the truck out for a preliminary test drive around the base, all was going well when Don decided to check out the 4 wheel drive system and proceeded to go into a rather large mony (monsoon) drain next to the road, no problems when going in, but when coming up the other side the back of the truck dug into the wall of the drain and literally suspended the back wheels off the ground, the front wheels didn't have enough traction to pull the truck out, so we were stranded. The water tank was full, with around 3000 litres of water, we tried emptying the tank and it seemed to help, but the truck was well dug in and still couldn't move.

No mobile phones in those days, so I was sent off on foot back to the workshop, only about 1km away, to organise a crane to lift it out.

It took a while for Don to live down the embarrassment, there are no cover-ups when things like this happen, it went into the book of "stuff ups" for the end of year presento's.

Truck Fire General Purpose (TFGP)

There was an occasion when our CO (Commanding Officer) came to us complaining that his car was misfiring around 110 KPH, and could we have a look at it. So Don and I found a road at the back of the base where we thought we could test it without worrying anyone, but the Service Police were on the ball and pulled us over doing 110 KPH, when the base speed limit was only 40 KPH, here we go how to explain this?.

Don told them the story, which they seemed to accept and all they said was, next time do it somewhere off base. There were some red faces and nervous laughter after they left; I don't think we'll do that again said Don.

There was interest amongst the troops with badminton; we had a court marked out on the hangar floor along with a net that we would set up every lunch time. Singles or doubles would be played depending on how many guys were around, rotating on a first come first play system, the matches could become very intense as some players acted as if they had sheep stations riding on the outcome, especially when the person they were playing alongside missed the shuttle cock. There were some who had good quality racquets and some who used the cheap ones that the social club supplied, mine had a hollow steel shaft that was supposed to be for strength, but I managed to break it in half. I repaired it by gluing a small steel rod inside the two halves, this worked but it made a rattling sound every time I hit the shuttle cock, making for some laughs from players and onlookers alike.

Another lunchtime game was darts where heckling the players was enjoyed by some, to the extent where I was the subject of one of these guys at one stage being "Nico", one of my young colleagues where I warned him to shut up or I'll throw a dart at him, he had at his defence a garbage can lid and thank his lucky stars he did as he had to use it, he just wouldn't shut up.

Unlike working in a civilian job and having cleaners that would do all the domestic cleaning, our junior ranks had extra duties which included cleaning the offices and lunch rooms, visiting the mess and bringing back food stuff, such as soup which was made from the day before left overs, milk, bread and whatever else was available, these duties were on a rotational basis.

Being in the automotive stream the fitters had an informal agreement with the cooks, where we would maintain their cars in exchange for certain food supplies for our social club events.

Other personnel needing repairs would pay with slabs of beer and or soft drinks, again for the social club, this was the accepted method of payment for any job done on base.

At this time spare parts would be ordered via microfiche "fiche" cards, these were small film like cards around 150mm x 100mm with many stock (part) numbers on them and when put in a viewing machine the numbers would be magnified.

Along with the stock numbers there would be a condensed description and unit of issue i.e. box, carton etc. Many occasions arose when the wrong unit of issue was used mainly with things like nuts and bolts, fittings etc. maybe we needed 100 nuts of a particular size for example and found what was thought to be the stock number for a box containing 50 nuts, but mistakenly it was the stock number for a carton of boxes and we would receive 2 cartons instead of 2 boxes, containing 100 boxes each, the part numbers where very similar and close together and sometimes hard to distinguish one from the other, this would happen time to time with similar outcomes.

This order would comprise many other items that would replenish our consumable supplies.

No questions were asked about the order and so our request would be filled and pallets of nuts and bolts would be delivered to our workshop, literally thousands of nuts and bolts with nowhere to put them, the equipment section didn't want to process the paperwork to send them back so we had to find somewhere to keep them.

Normally after a while the boss would tell us to take whatever was of use to us and bin the rest, what a waste.

The RAAF had its own stores depots back then and had or could get anything that had a stock number; this numbering system was worldwide and enabled procurement of almost anything.

There were limits to what sort of items each section could order, but there have been requisitions for rifles and aircraft parts right up to complete aircraft just to see how far the item would get before someone queried it, somehow I don't think the fitters really need an SLR rifle or an F111 bomber.

On one side of my hangar was the machine shop, where we had all the lathes, milling machines, welders etc. I think the only association with this section for me at this time was when I helped manoeuvre huge sheets of steel in and out of the steel racks, when the general fitters were building or fixing a piece of equipment.

I was licensed to operate a low profile Coles crane that had a clamp fitted to the lifting block, that would automatically grab hold of a sheet of metal once positioned correctly, this would enable me to lift it out of the steel rack and take it to where ever they wanted, I became very efficient with this crane and jump in whenever it was needed.

On the other side of the hangar was 9SQN (9Squadron), which comprised of from what I can remember approximately 12 UH-1 Iroquois helicopters or "Huey's" and 1 Search and Rescue helicopter (SAR) also an Iroquois. I can remember when all of them would be hovering on the flight line ready to taxi down to their dispatch area, how noisy they were and hoping no one would ring up my hangar as it would be impossible to carry out a conversation.

At times, just after the grass had been mowed around the area, the Huey's would start up and it would all be blown into our hangar and made an awful mess. They were magnificent to watch as one by one they would move off following each other, then taking off into the distance, only to come back a short time later in arrow head formation over the air field.

Huey's in formation at RAAF Amberley

Every so often they carried out training missions near the base, where they required volunteers to be part of the crew and I was lucky enough to be asked to participate.

I was briefed on what my role entailed along with a safety brief and fitted up with a helmet.

My role was to be winched down to the ground while the chopper hovered 30 metres or so off the ground, unhitch myself from the winch harness, walk over to some cement filled 205 litre oil drums, where the chopper would come overhead, and I would connect a lifting strap from one of the oil drums to the lifting hook on the belly of the chopper, I would then get clear and the chopper would lift it and set it back down again where I would unhitch the strap, this was to familiarise the pilot with lifting a weight and to test the load capacity of the chopper.

Imagine being under the belly of a chopper while it comes down over the top of you, you are nearly being blown off your feet, and the noise is immense as you are lifting the strap up and hooking it onto the chopper, once done giving thumbs up to the crew member watching from above, always remembering the words from the safety brief "if you see any signs of the chopper losing control hit the deck at the base of the drums".

Once this was carried out they would then do their low level flying and auto gyrating (emergency landing), as they couldn't do that with passengers, returning to winch me back up into the chopper on their return. This was an exciting experience, one I'll never forget, but I also remember the harness that was used for winching was positioned around my lower back, where the entire weight of my lower body hung off it and that was quite painful after a few minutes.

At one stage due to a natural disaster which I think was a Tsunami, affecting a neighbouring island which one I'm not sure, there were a number of GM diesel powered 45KVA generators flown into RAAF Amberley from around Australia, these could be linked up together through a control unit, and consequently sent out as a set to the affected area, enabling sufficient power to be restored. Being trained on these particular engines I worked alongside the electricians and would tune the engines to run together as one, enabling a steady power output.

Prior to this I had the job of picking the generators up from air movements, the main area where all aircraft operations were carried out, with a heavy duty forklift of which I had no previous experience; actually I had little experience with any forklift at that time. I think the use of the forklift was arranged prior to being picked up and I wasn't questioned about having a license to drive one then. I did know they had to be driven in reverse for safety and had a gear lever for forward and reverse, but I think this one had pedals for direction of travel.

It was confusing at first trying to work out the controls and I remember someone coming over to me and asking if I had a license and of course I lied and said yes, I just haven't come across these controls before. Anyway I managed to drive it down to where the generators were, and with the guidance of the guys there I was able to load the first one up.

The generators were huge and I couldn't see anything in front of me once it was loaded, now for the slow reverse trip back to my hangar (forklifts were driven in reverse when loaded up). There were a few "T" junctions to manoeuvre through before getting onto the main drag then a roundabout further down the road, I had to take it extra careful, if I had an accident I would be toast, not being licenced.

As time went on I became more proficient, picking up from what I remember 6 of them; I also remember having a very sore neck after from all the looking back, but it was great fun.

At one stage I had to have some extensive work done on my teeth and this was performed by a RAAF trained Dentist, meaning they carried out their training while being a member of the RAAF, not having any civilian experience prior, this they gained with us once they were qualified, at least that was my impression at the time.

After many visits and trauma preparing a particular tooth for a gold crown the time finally came to have it fitted, as most will be aware the adhesive that is used is ultra-quick setting, well the inevitable happened and it was incorrectly positioned so the dentist tried to remove it before it was set in place, he was able to remove it, but the post that was set in my tooth earlier also came out with it leaving a giant hole, I think he nearly fainted when that happened. Eventually he decided to temporarily fill it and have me come back at a later time to have another go, it was eventually done correctly and I still have it today.

In those days on pay day we were paid in cash and would have to attend a pay parade every fortnight, where we lined up at the door of the allocated office. The procedure was to approach the first desk, come to attention stating our name and service number, then given our pay packet, move to the side and count our pay, we would then go to another desk salute, and state "pay correct Sir" and sign for it, I don't recall ever having a problem. There were procedures if it wasn't correct, but I can't remember what they were, I imagine we would have to state our case or fill out a form stating the discrepancy and it would be looked into. We had allocated pay sections, were we would report to for other payments such as travel allowances and other miscellaneous payments, I expect we would report there if we had pay related enquires also. It wasn't unusual for wives of members to be waiting outside to collect their pay for shopping, banking etc.

In those days MTFITT's, were the only technical mustering that wore berets, I guess this was due to the nature of our job, being more appropriate if we were to get under a vehicle, where it wouldn't be appropriate for a service hat, and we were able to wash them, I always thought it was cool wearing these.

I mentioned earlier about having extra duties, we also had duties that extended to afterhours.

Most personnel would carry out some sort of out of hour's duties rostered throughout the year. This could include guard duty, duty Corporal, Sergeant or Officer at the relevant messes as well as other duties; my mustering would be rostered to carry out the role of Duty Ambulance Driver.

This was a sleeping duty, although not much sleep was to be had. We were to drive the crash ambulance in the event of a PAN (similar to mayday) or aircraft emergency. The F111 based at RAAF Base Amberley were known for their very touchy warning systems; never the less all were obviously taken seriously. An emergency could happen at any time aircraft were in the air, and many would be in the evening up to 2300 hrs when all aircraft activity was finished for the night.

The job was to front up to medical section after a normal work day, dressed in nicely pressed overalls ready for the night's duty. Medical section would use the duty ambulance driver to pick up the meals from the mess for personnel admitted into the wards, as well as our own; this was done as soon as we arrived, then it was a matter of sit and wait. The ambulance we used was based on a similar chassis to the TFGP fire truck and was fitted with an automatic gearbox, which was very unforgiving and would bang as it changed gear, no smooth changes here. The waiting was very nerve racking as the alarm bells could sound anytime.

On one such an occasion when I was on duty the alarm bells sounded, very loudly, I might add, It shocked the hell out of me, I ran out to the ambulance and drove it around to the front of the hospital to pick up the duty doctor and nurse, then drove like a mad man (probably no real need, but exciting none the less) with lights flashing and sirens wailing, banging through gears down to the control tower, where we waited with the other emergency crews (fire crew and barrier crew).

Once the aircraft landed it proceeded to pull up using its brakes as in a normal landing. It has been known for aircraft wheels to burst into flames due to the heat generated in the event of an emergency landing (the wheels are made of magnesium, a flammable metal). There is an emergency hook at the rear of the aircraft that hooks onto a cable on the runway if needed to slow it down; this wasn't used on this occasion, I will elaborate on this at a later stage. I chased it down the runway, it was after sundown and we were on the pitch black tarmac, the only lights available were the pathetic truck lights and the blue runway marker lights, which made for an eerie atmosphere.

I recall seeing 80 MPH on the speedo, then it came time to hit the brakes, both feet on the brake pedal, nearly pulling the steering wheel off to keep pressure on the brakes and just managed to stop near the aircraft, too bad if something ran out in front of me in the meantime, talk about an adrenaline rush, Phew, everyone was OK, no need for medical assistance this time. Back to medical and on alert for any other instances. There were a few similar emergencies during my time at RAAF Base Amberley, but always on edge ready for the adrenaline rush.

Continuing on from equipment that we "relived" we also had a fleet of 30,000 litre refuelling tankers. One of the procedures that these tankers had to undergo periodically was the bleaching of the epoxy coating on the inner walls, to kill off any microbiological organisms that may be living there. This same epoxy coating had a life span where it would be replaced at an external agency and would also be bleached before being returned to service.

To carry out the bleaching the tanker would be bought to an area just outside the hangar, where 2 of us dressed in overalls and wearing breathing apparatus and from what I can remember no boots only socks, would enter the tanker with the bleach solution and many lint free rags, as well as explosion proof lighting and proceed to wipe on, wipe off every part of the inner surface of the tanker.

There were many baffles and fittings throughout the tanker and getting to some parts was fiddly, but everything had to be cleaned. The tanker I have in mind from memory was one huge compartment although I may be wrong as others that I have experience with were divided into 4 separate tanks. This job took a while as we were timed and would come out on regular intervals to rehydrate and cool off.

Being out in the sun, the tankers would heat up considerably; we were monitored by a spotter at all times and would rotate with them throughout the process. Once finished an independent inspection was carried out, this was one of my least favourite jobs, so hot and claustrophobic.

Along the lines of least favourable jobs was when I had to take my turn in the Maintenance Control Section (MCS), located in the main 3AD headquarters building. All LAC's would rotate through here on a 6 monthly rotation, this is where all the paperwork regarding our work flow was generated, some printed by dot matrix printers, others by hand and returned here once completed, then filed away into log books (A4 folders), one for each piece of equipment that we looked after. This section was used by all trades in 3AD that had similar filing systems.

Every section on base would have at their disposal official publications relating to the equipment they worked with or maintained, as well as extensive publications regarding the overall running of the Air Force, from time to time these publications would have changes made known as amendments, rather than replacing the whole publication the affected pages would be replaced. It would be the daily job of the LAC MTFITT in MCS to deliver these amendments, along with other documentation, to all the sections of 3AD by hand and on foot. Some days the mail bag could be full, other days just a few or none, man what a pain.

3AD stretched for at least 1.5km and some of the sections were in obscure locations, we would do this in any weather, I remember wearing a jumper and jacket or rain coat in the cooler months. Another job particular to the MTFITT (because we held a defence driving license) was driving the Warrant Officer in charge of MCS to Bell Helicopters, near Brisbane, every Friday for a meeting, this made a nice break from the hum drum of work.

The RAAF ran on traditions and some no one could escape so it didn't matter who you were.

On one occasion when our Commanding Officer was discharging from the RAAF, we invited him down to our section to check out "something of interest" before he left.

We had a cherry picker work platform organised for him so he could get a good view of what we about to "show" him, being a little wise and luckily good humoured, removed his watch, wallet and pens from his pockets before we raised the platform several metres off the ground, where we turned the engine off. Around the corner of the hangar appeared a fire truck, with sirens blaring and lights flashing, proceeding to give our boss a good soaking before we lowered the work platform back down and offered him towels, our way of showing our appreciation for his leadership.

At the end of the year GEMS would provide a barbecue lunch where the management; Sergeants and above, would serve the lower ranks as a token of their thanks for the work done throughout the year, and at that lunch there would also be the issuing of "presento's" or "stuff up awards". These were plaques or certificates commemorating events where maybe a job didn't quite come out as expected, maybe something was broken or damaged in a memorable way, or something that was just worthy of an award, such as the fire truck that was jammed in the monsoon drain. This was represented by a small toy fire truck that was slightly broken in half and mounted on a plaque, suitably representing the deed, not many escaped being put in the book for these awards. I'm not sure if other sections on the base had this sort of celebration, but I do know it was carried out at GEMS across Australia.

Time marches on and we had our second baby girl, Toni-Rae, on 03 August, 1982 our "RAAF brat" as children born while having a parent/s in the RAAF were affectionately known.

I rode a motorbike (actually I had a few different bikes while I was at RAAF Amberley) to work at that time and remember when the girls were old enough, when I came home from work, they would scramble onto it and I would take them up and down the nature strip, Toni-Rae between me and the tank and Kristy hanging on behind me, they loved it.

One of the bikes I owned was a Suzuki DR 500 trail bike which I took out on the trails not far from where we lived where I came across a burnt out mini on its roof, obviously stolen by some of the local hooligans, so I stopped and checked it over for spare parts for my mini, I didn't find anything worth keeping except for a set of wheel spacers. These went between the brake drums and wheels moving them out 25mm each side, giving it a wider wheel base.

Things were going great, really enjoying the job, the kids were happy, but apparently my wife wasn't. My life was about to undergo a devastating upheaval, out of nowhere in 1984, I was dumped for another man. This meant among other things, like my girls being taken away from me, I had to surrender the married quarters and find somewhere else to live.

I didn't like the idea of living in single men's quarters on base, this accommodation was ok for young single guys who liked running amok, but it was too confined for me. I think there were two men to a room in huge buildings with many floors, and having to share ablutions and laundry facilities with 20 to 30 others per floor. I found a share house off base that suited me better.

I was gutted at this stage after having my family taken away from me, and becoming single again, when a posting came along not too far from Amberley at a small town in Northern NSW known as Evans Head.

"Presento" from 3AD on posting

I was given a send-off of some kind, but I can't remember what, but I do still have my first "Presento", commemorating my first posting. This posting was a great way to start my RAAF career, where I met a lot of good people and shared some great experiences.

Chapter 3
Posted to Evans Head

THE POSTING TO EVANS Head seemed timely as I needed to gather my thoughts away from where it all went wrong. I rode my motorcycle (a Kawasaki GPZ 750) down to Evans Head before I was posted there, to see where it was and what it was like.

My GPZ 1984 750

In WWII, Evans Head airport originally supported RAAF No 1 Bombing and Gunnery School (1BAGS). It seemed great, located off the main highway by about 6km's on the coast with no through road. Evans Head is home to a practice bombing range, which is located approximately 4km's in national park land from the town.

Soon after the visit my posting date came up, so I packed up the few possessions I had left at that time and drove my car down, I had organised a lift back to Amberley shortly after to pick up my motorcycle. The local Motel served as single man's quarters at that stage, with a large room at the front of the building serving as my room, a little later on I was able to move into a private unit located on "snob hill", so named due to being the more expensive side of town.

As a single man I would pay for rations and quarters, where the Motel was my quarters and the facilities in town would supply rations. These facilities were the RSL, the Chinese restaurant at the motel, the local butcher and the pub. These businesses would send their bills to the Motel, as the RAAF would send an allowance to the Motel to cover our (singlies) expenses, and on a monthly basis the Motel management would pay us the balance if there was any left. I'm not sure if they were supposed to, but they did anyway and that was greatly appreciated.

There was a tradition at the pub where a mini beer stein was kept, named "Truckies mug" "Truckie" being the nick name given to the fitter. The idea was when a new MTFITT started there he would be asked what his favourite spirit was, the beer stein was then filled with whatever spirit he had nominated and he was to drink it all before the night was out (approximately 2 hours), this was no mean feat especially when I wasn't particularly a drinker.

Life was fairly lay back here at Evans Head, I spent my evenings and sometimes weekends down at the pub, RSL club or bowls club, meeting up with friends and having a few drinks.

Other than that, I would go on long rides on my motor bike, quite often with one of the local girls on the back, being only 1 hour from Surfers Paradise; this was always on the cards.

Spending time on the beach was always an option, enjoying the crashing of the 6ft waves, something you never get tired of.

The bombing range was manned by 6 people; the boss was a Flight Lieutenant (from my experience a pilot who was now flying a desk), then a SGT Armament Fitter (Gunnie), an Lac MTFITT and 3 General hands. The main objective of the bombing range is to maintain an area for pilots to practice and hone their bombing and gunnery skills. During WWII live bombing also took place here, that section is now disused and fenced off due to some unexploded bombs still buried and out of reach due to tidal movement at the bomb site. These bombs are known and are monitored by bomb disposal experts.

Before they fenced it off I witnessed the destruction of one bomb that came close enough to the surface to have the mud cleared away from around it, enabling the bomb disposal team to detonate a charge of C4 and consequently destroying it, what a blast.

We had 2 4wd's that we used to take us out to the range every morning, the first vehicle would leave approximately 15 minutes earlier and would get the range up and running.

Access to the range was via tick gates; these gates were a part of a dual fence line running through the bush and out to sea, there would be gates across all the roads on the fence line.

This is where during the 1950s to 1970 vehicles carrying cattle would be checked for ticks, attempting to stop the movement of ticks from north to south.

Our gates were still operational for security reasons. There were multiple locks linked together on the gates, as different departments had access to the National Park and would have their own lock.

I remember one morning when pathetically attempting to unlock one of our locks, I said to Sammy our SGT who was driving, if you see me doing anything strange today, it's because I shared a smoke with one of the girls in town last night, I think it was laced with something and I'm not myself this morning, he just laughed and said "can't you take a joke", that made me feel a little better about myself.

The boss had a direct line to RAAF Amberley at his home address, and would be notified when to expect the first aircraft of the day, he would be the one to pick up the remainder of the crew after the guys opening the range had left. I would normally be one of these guys while living at the hotel, along with "beach ball" one of the General Hands, aptly named due to his body shape, lovely guy. We would wait outside the hotel at the prescribed time, for some days up to 1 hour or more, as the boss liked to cut it as close as possible and we had no clue of when to expect him, his nick name, unknown to him at the time as far as we knew was "splinter" as he got under everyone's skin, even the locals knew him as such.

Before any bombing would commence and on the way out to the range, red flags were deployed at key areas (jetties etc.) notifying the public that bombing was going ahead that day. We would also carry out a beach clearance run with one of the 4WD's along the coastal area of the range, where anyone on that part of the beach fishing or swimming would be put in the vehicle and taken to the specified safe zone closer to town.

There wasn't any town power on site so we would have to power up our own diesel generator, and if there was to be morning bombing we also had to power up the generator at the remote quadrant, on our way; this was a facility that housed a camera facing south and sent a signal via microwave to the main tower. This camera feed was used in by the scoring equipment; there was also a camera at the main tower that faced east, with these two cameras' we would be able to plot where a bomb landed.

At this stage I hadn't experienced any of this, so completely new. I had completed a course however on how to use the bomb scoring equipment, but that doesn't really equip you with everything needed to carry out the job. Fortunately there is a period of hand over take over, where the fitter I was taking over from was still at the range and would show me the ropes, as it were.

I had met everyone I was to be working with earlier in town, now was the time to learn everything at the range. After a quick once around of all the equipment I would be running and maintaining, it was time to experience my first bombing run. The pilot or pilots depending on how many were in circuit would correspond via radio; we could only listen where the boss could talk to the pilots when necessary.

It took a while to understand what was being said over the radio as the pitch was different to that of normal speech. We could see the aircraft in the distance; they would approach from different angles of attack and that would be selected on the scoring equipment once radioed in. The main aircraft that were using the range at that time were F111 (F one eleven) fighter bomber's from RAAF Amberley; visiting aircraft would also use the range occasionally when joint exercises were taking place in the region.

The 25lb practice bomb they released would represent a group of 500lb bombs. There were two different targets; one for visual sighting and the other for radar sighting, where the aircrafts on-board radar system could determine the location of the target by reflecting signals off reflectors situated around the target.

When the bomb hit the ground a smoke flare would be activated in the tail, this could be seen on the screens of the scoring equipment, and the personnel operating it would move a cursor on the screen corresponding to the flare via a dial and press the send button. The coordinates of the bomb were then sent to the boss sitting upstairs in the tower, he would then radio that information to the pilot.

An F111 pulling up after a bombing run

There were two shifts a day, 0800hrs to 1600hrs and coming back to the base at 1900hrs for night bombing, finishing at 2300hrs, same procedures, but instead of a smoke flare all we would see was a flash, this could be missed if full attention wasn't payed to the screens (sometimes conversations could get a little rowdy and focus could be diverted), luckily the flash would linger faintly on the screens for a short time enabling us to back track where it landed.

The whole procedure would become intense when up to 5 or 6 aircraft were in circuit, having to change Aircraft tail no's and attack modes on the scoring equipment each time a jet came through, this involved the four of us, two manning the scoring equipment and the other two manually spotting the aircraft (no conversations at this time).

All of the general hands and I would be involved in bomb scoring and maintenance of the various fences and targets on the base, where I would be responsible for repair and maintenance of the vehicles and various generators and other mechanical equipment.

Even though red flags were deployed, and information regarding the operation of the bombing range was widely disseminated, we would still encounter the odd sailing ship or fishing boat in the waters off the coast of the range, and consequently bombing would not commence until they were clear. We had no direct way of communicating with these boats so we would ask a jet to fly directly at them, pulling up and over hoping to give them the message, sometimes having to do it more than once. We would wonder if they did this for the rush and the photo opportunity or were genuinely ignorant.

An F4 Phantom beating up an unwelcome yacht while on exercise at Evans Head

At times we would encounter 4wd's taking off from the beach, as they saw our vehicle approaching while carrying out a beach sweep. Even though we had 5 feet high barbed wire fences at either end of the bombing zone, high seas at times would wash sand up sufficiently to cover the fences and the 4wd's would drive over. These people were taking the opportunity to fish in normally unfished waters due to the no go zone of the bombing range.

When all maintenance was up to speed and no aircraft around, some of us were able to participate in our hobbies. One of the General Hands (GH), Ian was an avid blacksmith who had a forge set up outside of the workshop, and would make various items using the skills his grandfather taught him. Gary, another GH was a qualified electrician before he joined the RAAF and was looking for a change of pace, I'm not sure if he had a hobby, but he was always busy.

I rebuilt a 1974 Leyland Mini in the new workshop which had just been erected before I arrived; I also repainted it changing the colour to gunmetal grey with gold metal flake over the top. I'm not sure what Sammy the SGT or the Boss got up to in the quiet periods.

"Beach ball" had a small armoury of his own, with a stash of weapons in an appropriate locker stored on base, he reloaded his own ammunition, allowing him to vary loads if he chose to do so. I remember him owning a couple of big bore hand guns, short and long barrel, a Special Purpose Automatic Shot Gun (SPAS), this was a piece of work, able to shoot from the hip with little recoil, along with some other rifles.

We would set up targets in our rubbish dump area behind the base, and fire these weapons along with our service rifle (SLR), and sometimes when the local copper came out for a visit we would also shoot his service revolver. A great day would be had by all, even with a hangover, just ask the copper ha ha.

Some nights when things were slow we would shoot at the bombing targets with our SLR service rifle, one target was shaped as a pyramid with a floodlight on the top, the aim was to shoot the floodlight out, this was at least 300metres away, I don't recall this ever happening other than some ricochets close to it .

Tracer rounds would be used, these are bullets coated with a small pyrotechnic mixture in their base causing it to burn brightly when fired. These were collected after the Huey gunships (so named due to the model No. of the chopper being HU-1) that came to the range for gunnery practice, had left. Some bullets were found on the ground where the Huey's had flown i.e. when the trigger of the mini gun was released some live rounds would be lost out of the ejection port due to the momentum of the barrels, others were from ends of belts given to us when the exercise was finished, these were the same calibre rounds used in the SLR; it was amazing seeing the trajectory of a bullet as the phosphorus burnt on its way to the target, I had never witnessed anything like this before, other than on movies, and found it quite spectacular.

Talking of Huey Gunships; 9SQN visited the range on one occasion while I was there, for a weekend exercise with two of their Huey gunships, these were armed with two fixed forward firing minigun (one each side) and a 7-round rocket pod on each side and the aircrew manned M60 machineguns on each door.

Huey Gunship Armament: M60 top, Minigun left, Rocket Launcher right

We had set up "mock villages" in an area designated on the range for the gunships to use as targets; I would imagine this was due to the fact that their last combat was during the Vietnam War. They would fly in figure 8 formations to enable both door gunners an opportunity to fire down range at the targets, I think only one was in circuit at any time. The rockets and Minigun were fired separately. The rockets had some sort of stainless steel lanyard (possibly an arming device) which would be in the path of the rocket flame, dropping to the ground glowing white hot and starting bush fires.

We had one of our 4WDs being a utility, configured for firefighting with a large capacity water tank and pump fitted to the back, along with two or three of us carrying back pack firefighting pumps. This was arduous, hot work; also being in the summer didn't make it any easier, great experience though.

A Huey gunship in circuit at Evans Head

A couple of Huey's coming to the range

Once finished firefighting and back at base we stripped down to our underwear and were being doused by the fire hose to cool off, when our

CO from RAAF Amberley arrived for a visit, not particularity the attire to greet him in, but due to his timing that's what he got, of course he understood and appreciated the situation.

The gunships carried out similar sessions at night, where a 1 million candle power flare was dropped from a Huey at a predetermined height lighting the whole area for approximately 3 minutes while they carried out their night firing, flares would be repeatedly dropped throughout the night. Due to the bright light of the flares they could be seen for miles, and apparently the police received calls regarding "UFO" sightings from the public.

A 1 million candle power flare over Evans Head

We still had the same problem regarding fires and being at night they were easily spotted, only problem being was the illusion of flat ground ahead, where in reality there were all sorts of hazards to account for e.g. trees and shrubs, undulating ground surfaces etc. The method we used was having one of us up front with a powerful flash light, which would be pointed ahead enabling him to see where we were going, and then swinging it behind him so the person behind could see what was coming up, doing this in quick succession we could navigate through the undergrowth to get to the fire, I remember seeing a low lying tree at crotch height come up just in time to jump it. Some of the land would fall away by metres, so you had to watch the path being struck by the man up front, this was done while carrying a 20ltr backpack fire pump sloshing away as you rushed through the bush.

One afternoon after manoeuvres, we were invited down to where the Huey's were temporarily stationed. The crew had set up one of the M60 machine guns on a free standing mount to enable us to experience the power of these beasts. Firing at targets around 200 metres away, these are fully automatic machine guns with spade grips at the rear and thumb triggers on either grip, fed by a belt of rounds which seemed endless, a powerful piece of kit. (Refer to pic. Huey Armament). The M60 had a rhythm of 'boof boof boof', whereas the Minigun sounded more like 'Brrrrrt' due to the rate of fire. The 9SQN crew were staying at the local motel for the duration of their exercise and from what I hear drank a little too much for the liking of the owners, (not unusual for SQN boys) and consequently this was to be their last sortie at Evans Head. I vaguely remember a Chinook aka "Chook" (twin rotor Chopper) from 12SQN coming down also at one stage, I think this had M60 machine guns in the doors and needed to test them out.

A Chinook with M60 machine guns in the doors visiting Evans Head

The F111 bombers also carried out gunnery at the range. We had a target area set up on one of the sand dunes; this was a regulated area that was routinely cleared of previously fired rounds, the possibility of ricochets may have occurred if not cleared, this was done using a tractor drawn device. Orange nets were used as targets due to the high visibility against the sand. The actual position of the rounds going through the net was measured by a parabolic microphone. The microphone could detect the rounds as they cracked the sound barrier near the microphone and recorded on a receiver in another location, these were interesting to setup, as everything at Evans Head, all new to me.

The gun used on the F111 aircraft was a single 6 barrel, 20mm M61 Vulcan, with the rate of fire at 6000 rounds per minute, using H.E. (high explosive) ammunition, but inert training rounds were used on the range with the trigger set to a 1 second burst, that would equate to a very quick brrrt. On one occasion during a gunnery run, one of the F111 in circuit pulled out of formation after firing, without any communication to us and from what we learned later, headed straight back to RAAF Amberley. Apparently there is a deflector plate fitted above the gun to guard the nose of the aircraft if a round goes astray, in this instance the plate wasn't fitted or incorrectly fitted and stray rounds destroyed the radar dish in the nose among other things, this could have accounted for the lack of communication.

A short time later the entire crew at Evans Head had to attend an F111 fireman's course held at RAAF Amberley and we were able to view the aircraft and the damage done and it was quite extensive, with many holes measuring around 30mm in the radar dish amongst other components, luckily they weren't live rounds, I was shocked when I saw the damage.

The course we attended possibly bought on by this incident, covered how the ejection system worked and the hazards/explosives we could encounter if the ejection module was deployed or an F111 went down at the range.

On occasion the Boss would request a low fly over aka "beat up", to celebrate a birthday or just for the hell of it, where an F111 would come over the tower with the wings swept back at a great rate of knots at what seemed only metres above us with an almighty roar.

I had my parents visiting the range on one occasion, when the USAF were using the range while on exercise with a squadron of, if I remember correctly, F4 phantoms, these planes had shark teeth painted on their nose and looked great.

F4 Phantom flying over Evans Head

A request was put to them to carry out a "beat up" and I think there were 3 of them in tight formation come over. Needless to say my parents and everyone else there at the time were impressed, a big Thank You was sent to them over the radio as they disappeared into the distance.

When I first started working at Evans Head, Friday was deemed a maintenance day and there was normally no flying except on the odd occasion, but under the boss at that time it was proclaimed a no work day, therefore a 3-day weekend was had by all, but things were to change about 10 months later, when there was a new boss in town who didn't seem so pleased about being posted to Evans Head, I did hear that this was due to some sort of flying incident which put him behind a desk? We lost our long weekend and things became a little tighter, but that wasn't such a bad thing, at least we had more direction and a short time later our new boss started to relax, after all we were working in our own little paradise.

Our camping site at the range.

A recreation come camping site was set up behind the sand dunes where friends and family would be invited to come and enjoy our "private" beach. Sometimes when down at the camping site, I would have my off road trike there for anyone who would like to take it for a ride, it was the type with big balloon tires in lieu of suspension and was powered with a 250 motorbike engine. Most would take it over the sand dunes to the beach, it was comical to watch as they put their foot down to the ground when traversing the dune like you would if on a motorbike to keep it from falling over, totally forgetting it was a three wheeler and to their surprise the back wheel, which was now perfectly lined up with their leg, would in effect attempt to ride up it and scare the hell out of them, no harm done other than a scuff mark on their calf.

The trike originally belonged to one of the General Hands and I bought it from him soon after I arrived at the range, the only fault I found with it was difficulty changing gears until it was warmed up, this was due to the wrong oil being put in the engine for the clutch to work properly when cold.

Scattered around the buildings were mementos of days gone by, and one that stuck out because of its size as well as the statement it made, was a 500lb inert bomb sitting at the base of the tower, representing what we were doing there in the first place. To work here was an honour as only a few would get the opportunity to experience what is essentially the final product, as it were, of all the hard work a huge team contribute to.

A 500lb bomb situated on the lawn area at the base of the tower

In those days upon initial enlistment we signed up for a 6 year contract, and the time was fast approaching where a decision had to be made whether to stay or leave. I had decided to leave even though I had a great posting in Evans Head, but that wasn't going to last forever sad to say, sometimes sacrifices have to be made. This decision was mainly due to the fact that I was suffering from my marriage breakup, and also I was a little stale with the pace and my progress in the RAAF.

A change was needed and I was looking forward to the fast pace of civilian employment, I elected to be discharged back home to Hobart, but seeing there wasn't a base in Hobart, I would have to be discharged at the nearest one and that was RAAF Laverton, 1AD GEMS (Ground Equipment Maintenance Section) near Melbourne in Victoria.

For my send off at Evans the guys arranged a get together at the pub, where some of the towns people that I got to know during my posting attended, along with the RAAF crew.

I don't particularly remember much about it other than going back to my room at the hotel, with one of the girls from the pub both of us on her bicycle; how we managed I don't know.

As well as the send-off I was presented with a Pewter tankard from the crew to commemorate my stay.

Pewter Tankard "Presento"

Chapter 4

1AD GEMS and my discharge

I DROVE DOWN TO MELBOURNE the next day in the Mini, where my other possessions along with my motorbike were being shipped down soon after. There was a period of 4 months to be spent at RAAF Base Laverton before my discharge was finalised and that was to be 22 September, 1986.

As far as I can remember, I didn't know anyone at this base, but that wasn't a problem as I found it easy to form working and social relationships with the new crew, as well as the equipment and type of work being more or less the same as 3AD giving all a commonality.

As I didn't have a nickname at the time, one of the guys I worked with decided to call me "Chuckles", I asked why and he said, because you always have a smile on your face even when things aren't so good. This seemed to be the sentiment shared by the majority of my work mates; I thought fair enough, at least I know how I'm seen by my fellow workers.

The on base accommodation, where I was to live temporarily, happened to be a little more up to date compared to the large blocks available at RAAF Base Amberley. It consisted of condo style buildings, each comprising 3 or 4 floors, having 5 or so rooms to a floor, sharing a common room and a couple of bathrooms, one at each end of the rooms, as well as a laundry, it was also unisex. I remember one night after some of us that lived on base had come back from a night on the town, when one of the guys came back out of his room stunned, muttering something about a girl curled up at the foot of his bed.

It turned out that one of the girls that lived on the level above us, had been to the on base boozer and after having a few too many drinks, returned to what she thought was her room (how she managed to get in the room is a mystery), curling up on the foot of the bed and falling asleep. We all thought it was a great joke, but kept quiet so as not to wake her.

I think the guy whose room it was, slept on the couch in the common room that night, the girl must have woke some time during the night and realised her mistake and slipped back to her room, so funny.

It just so happened that one of the guys I went through rookies with was also leaving the RAAF from here as well, he had been in the same unit for the entire length of his enlistment, I think he was a Clerk Supplier or similar. His co-workers had organised lunch at a strip joint to send him off and he invited me along to share the fun, telling me this is your send-off too, which I greatly appreciated.

As a parting gift the motor trimmer working at GEMS, installed a black vinyl roof onto my mini and the painter offered to give it an additional coat of clear, as it was still a little rough from where I applied the gold metal flake when in Evans Head, of course I gladly accepted, I also asked if he could tint the clear coat with a touch of black to give it some depth, of which he obliged saying that he would have to use the whole 4 litres, because he couldn't use it for anything else, oh well shame about that.

My 1974 Mini Clubman

Also as a parting gift, one of the General Fitters who I worked alongside said to back my mini into the workshop, and he proceeded to fill the boot with all sorts of small tools such as drill bits, taps and dies and anything he could get his hands on, these lasted me for years after I left.

On my departure I was paid out the money which had been taken out of my pay (5.5%) over the years, by the way of Defence Force Retirement and Death Benefits (DFRDB) contributions, but because I hadn't reached any particular qualifying period (i.e. 20yr's in service) it didn't gain any interest. Soon after all this I was to drive to the ferry at Port Melbourne that would take me back home to Hobart, again my possessions and motorbike were shipped soon after.

"Presento" from 1AD

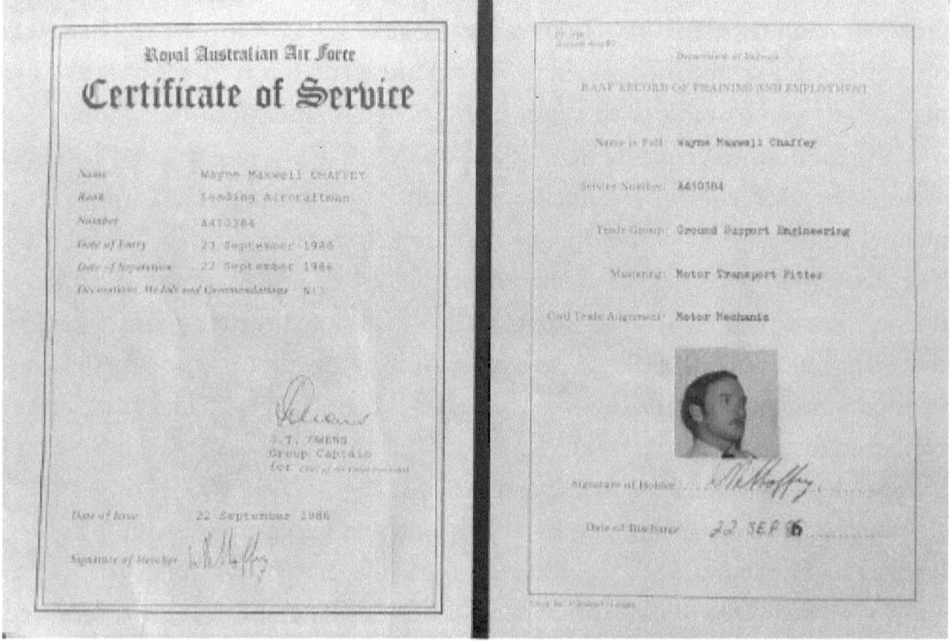

Certificate of Service upon discharge in 1986

Return to Hobart

So I arrived back in Hobart, living with Mum and Dad and trying to fit back into the civilian world. It was great to be with my parents again and being able to do odd jobs around the house for them. They gave me the room under the house, allowing me to have my own space, even though I had to come up to the main house for everything except sleeping.

Soon after my arrival, I managed to find a job as a motor mechanic at a service station in the suburb of Glenorchy, this being on the western side of Hobart with an apprentice under my control; it was interesting work at times, having to come up with innovative ways to keep cars on the road without having to charge too much.

At that time it was the only servo in the area that was offering full driveway service, this called for whoever was serving the customer, to manually ring up their transaction and take back the change. At the end of the day during rush hour when everyone was on their way home, I had to down tools and join the crew servicing the driveway. This was way out of my comfort zone, there was only one cash register and we had to wait in line to do our transactions, I wasn't particularly comfortable with handling money so no mistakes.

The predominant payment method was cash in those days, and if credit cards were used the only available method of processing them was with a manual credit card machine. At one stage I remember a customer telling me I had given him the change for a ten dollar note, when he had given me a twenty dollar note, this of course was incorrect, he was told by the owner of the servo that he would have to wait till the close of business that day, when the days takings were counted and put against what the cash register had rung up, of course no discrepancy was found, he lucked out this time, bastard. After a while I found this job to be tiresome, so I moved on.

During the next 15 months or so I had a few different jobs including going back up to Northern NSW near Evans Head, due to the laws in NSW I had to apply for a license to work, from what I understand the only state that required a license for motor mechanics at the time.

To obtain the license I had to prove I was qualified, but unfortunately seeing that I had failed a calculation exam during my apprenticeship, I was not issued a certificate, this exam was removed from the syllabus the following year, no help to me though. I was to either sit the same exam at the local Tech College or join the IAME, (Institute of Automotive Mechanical Engineers) where I would have to pass a 100 question exam. With the help of the Tech College we found the correct exam, but same results; failure.

So I joined the IAME and passed their exam, all this to only work in NSW for a matter of months, as I moved back to Hobart shortly afterwards. I found a position in a small workshop in the city; it was ok, but a little boring.

It took the entire time I was back in civy street, to realise what I missed being in the RAAF. In a civilian position the prospects of advancement are very slim in my trade, whereas in the RAAF, advancement was always on the table through courses and promotion prospects, as well as ones working life being more exciting. It was now that I decided to reenlist, so being back in Hobart I visited the recruitment centre and found they were still in need of MTFITT's, I applied, was accepted and six months later was on my way, no need to go through rookies again and I retained my rank, but I did lose any seniority I had built up in my first enlistment.

Unknown to me at the time, if I had reenlisted 12 months or sooner after discharge I would have retained my seniority, but now I had to start at the bottom, oh well typical RAAF, a lot of information such as this is available just not communicated very well, this was upsetting, but what could I do.

I had elected to be posted to 492 SQN situated at RAAF Base Edinburgh this time working at the "sharp" end. This choice was made due to the fact that my daughters were living close by giving me a chance to be their Dad again. I gave my then boss 3 week's notice, thinking I would be able to stay working for him until I left for the RAAF, but not the case, he found someone else very quickly and put me off a week later, so much for doing the right thing, that really pissed me off. My father said to me "you'll be able to make up the lost wages soon after you start back in the RAAF", that was true enough.

Chapter 5
My second reenlistment – RAAF Edinburgh

SO I ARRIVED IN ADELAIDE and started work on the 30 June, 1988, where I was reunited with some of my colleagues that I had worked with on my first enlistment. 492SQN is home to P3 Orion Maritime patrol Aircraft who carried out surveillance of Australia's coast. They were equipped with all sorts of sonar buoys and torpedoes depending on their mission at the time, along with the capability to listen for submarines.

P3 Orion

When I first fronted up to my new unit I was introduced to all concerned as was expected, when one of the Sergeants asked if I was going to buy back my previous time, I didn't know what he was talking about, turns out it was another situation with a procedure already in place, but not conveyed to members when it was of vital importance that they knew.

This lack of communication in the Defence Force was one of the few things that really irked me.

This enabled members who reenlisted to pay back their previous DFRDB contributions, either as a lump sum or gradually over the time it would take them to complete 20yrs service, this being a milestone where if a member was to elect discharge at this point in time, they would be eligible for a part pension. After hearing about this it was one of the first things I got under way.

I didn't know at the time, but this was to be my longest posting, 8 years in fact, as my girls were here I amplified my posting preferences to stay as long as I could.

There were a few different sections that 492GEMS was split into and I was relegated to Fire section on my arrival. This was the maintenance section, where we worked closely with the Fiery's on the flight line, mainly due to the large number of breakdowns that came from them, predominately from misuse of the equipment. As the water pressure used was very high, in the event a valve was opened or shut at the wrong time, with maximum pressure applied, it could do all sorts of damage, this was a worry.

At one stage one of our fitters had to supervise them when they carried out their daily checks, to ensure they were operating the equipment correctly.

While in fire section, the on base golf course was being established, and lacked any sort of watering system for the trees/shrubs that were being planted, so one of our jobs was to take an Oshkosh P4 fire truck, with a full tank (5000 litres) of water over to the golf course, and give everything a good watering once or twice a week.

Oshkosh P4 Fire Truck

There were a few variants to the fire truck fleet with the P4 being at the top of the list, their main role was to provide fire services in the case of aircraft emergencies, I'm not sure how many were available, but I should imagine 4-5 with 2 or 3 on line at any time, followed by International 4x4 early rescue truck's, TFGP's; the same fire truck that was overhauled in 3AD and water tanker's.

I remember travelling to RAAF Base Woomera to service a P4 fire truck that was positioned there at the time, the base is in the dessert, more or less in the middle of South Australia.

Woomera is known for its experimental rocket facility, as well as playing a part in the Atomic bomb tests in 1956 – 1963 at Maralinga.

I can't remember how the base was manned, but I think it had a civilian caretaker looking after it. From what I could work out, it was only operational during exercises.

Woomera is positioned approximately 800km North of Adelaide and at a certain point there was no speed limit imposed, making for more timely travel. Two of us were assigned to this task and we stayed overnight at "Aldo's", a small hotel that would cater for service personnel as well as anyone else travelling up that way. While there we explored some of the hangars on base and come across one full of retired "Mirages", a delta wing jet fighter the RAAF used before we took delivery of our F111's. This was a complete shock as we had heard no mention of this anywhere, maybe a secret that we stumbled across.

⎯⎯⎯ ❦ ⎯⎯⎯

Meanwhile, back at 492SQN.

Just like any other base some of the guys would get up to something a little unusual every now and then just for the hell of it, sometimes it would make you wonder what was on their mind , I will try to cover some of these antics as I remember them.

In spring we had a problem where many Plover's would nest and hatch their young all over the base, and look out if you were anywhere near that nest. The male Plover could do some major damage as it would swoop down and attack unsuspecting people, if they happened to be anywhere near the nest, this particular year we had one nest on the roof of the main hangar and the male Plover was swooping everyone in the vicinity of the building, so one of the guys (Bliz) decided he would be smart and sneak up on the nest using a cherry picker work platform. This was a self-propelled vehicle that had a hydraulic boom and a fully enclosed platform or basket at the end of it, making it very manoeuvrable and able to move in any direction.

He slowly approached the roof line, when he came face to face with the Plover who was waiting for him, the Plover immediately attacked, startling Bliz who nearly fell out of the cherry picker, creating a loud cheer from all watching on, he managed to ward it off and quickly lowered the cherry picker and got the hell out of there. I can't remember what happened next, I have an idea somehow or other the nest was moved to another location out of harm's way. Many people either jogging or riding bicycles around the base would be pestered by the Plovers, the joggers would carry sticks they would wave around above their heads in an attempt to deter the birds from attacking, the bike riders had helmets at least.

Our Warrant officer at the time was known to most personnel as "Grinner", due to the fact he would have a huge grin on his face all the time even when dressing us down.

This nick name would only be used among the troops, on account of it not being appreciated by the higher ranks due to it being a sign of disrespect, although they knew of it and would turn a deaf ear if they were to come across it. He was known for some strange behaviour though, for example; at times people would drive a bit too fast in the vicinity of the hangar where there was a speed limit of 10kph, causing a safety issue seeing it was a shared zone, so "Grinner" at times would hide in the bushes and jump out when someone drove past noticeably too quick and stop them.

I remember when we were on a Monday morning parade outside the hangar one time, (this was a full dress and bearing inspection) when one of the guys (Adam) let out a really disgusting stench, due to some strange diet he was on at the time, this nearly floored everyone, "Grinner" ordered him to go down to medical section and have them check him out, dry reaching as he spoke. Adam was known for his unusual dietary habits; yeah this wasn't especially strange behaviour, but forking funny. We had an expression for people in that situation, something like "I think you need to use the dead rat extractor".

The average rotation for section change was 6 months and my next move was to be light vehicle section, where the majority of vehicles were staff cars along with some of the smaller tow motors, (these were used mainly for towing trailers and generator sets etc.) and forklifts.

Speaking of tow motors, one of our "Domino" (model name) tow motors needed some major work done on its rear axle, this was my job, so I carried it out and upon putting it back together I asked my "independent inspector" (Grossy) to check everything before it was closed up, this is normal practice if a component is encased in some way and can't be accessed once put back together, he was happy with what he checked and I proceeded to finish off.

At the time neither of us realised the crown wheel (a major part of the differential) could be put in two different ways and still look and fit fine. One way would move the vehicle predominately backwards and the other way forward; I imagine this would allow the assembly to be used in other applications. I think you may have guessed where I'm heading with this, well the time came for a test drive, I put it in reverse to back out of the bay I was working in and totally unexpectedly it shot forward, you know, the same feeling when you think you put a car into reverse, but it's actually a forward gear, shocks the hell out of you.

I thought I accidently had it in the wrong gear, but no, that wasn't the case, you guessed it, I had 4 reverse gears and 1 forward, that being now in the same place where reverse would have been. Everyone around was cracking up including me, but when "Grossy" heard about it he came over with head down and muttering to himself. He took the responsibility as he gave his OK; this was hard for him to swallow as he had the reputation of being a stickler for details and was recently posted in from RAAF Wagga where he was an instructor, nether the less, farking funny.

We held all the hand tools we used on large central tool boards, having approximately 3 of every tool available, all the tools were "shadowed" as in a black representation of the tool painted on the board to allow easy identification when one was in use. Everyone had a number of round discs which were colour coded and numbered, referenced to our name and upon taking a tool we would hang a disc in its place. This would serve as tool control, as in the event a tool was missing from the board at the end of the day it would be traced to the person whose name was tagged against it, if it was not found in the workshop it could possibly be left in the vehicle that was worked on that day. Normally we wouldn't be allowed to leave the workshop until all tools were accounted for, at times tools would be left somewhere on a vehicle and that vehicle taken out onto the airfield, where the tool could fall off onto a taxiway or runway creating the possibility of Foreign Object Damage (FOD), this is where they could be sucked up into a jet engine destroying it. The personnel working on the flight line would have to do a FOD sweep every morning, by forming a line that would cover the whole area external to the hangars where aircraft would move over. They would move slowly forward, picking up anything that could cause FOD, if there was anything substantial found it would have to be reported e.g. nuts and bolts, lock wire, tools etc.

Around this time I had started body building again, I initially started when I was in Hobart and really enjoyed it. On my way home after work I would train in a civilian gym and occasionally at the base gym; my goal was to enter into a body building competition at some time in the future. A few of the guys I worked with were also into it and we would talk about techniques and diet a fair bit, at times we would train together at the base gym, we would get time during work hours occasionally as fitness was a requirement in the Defence Force.

During work I would incorporate some exercises into my work routine, such as when I was jacking a vehicle up or using a manual oil transfer pump.

When the time was right I entered a few competitions; the first one was a shambles as I didn't know what was required in the way of format, e.g. compulsory posing, where everyone would have to line up and together, strike a series of poses for the judges to compare each competitor, and after that have a routine set to their chosen music that would show the best aspects of their body. I didn't realise until I watched the group before me do their thing, my heart dropped and panic stations, I didn't go on stage when my group was called, I just watched and quietly left feeling disappointed and embarrassed, when the next opportunity came up I made sure I knew what to do.

Before I started body building I was fairly quiet and didn't have much of a presence, then after a while especially when I was reasonably serious about it, my body started changing and so did my confidence, the people I worked with were starting to take notice of me, and that made me feel more appreciated and respected, to this day I attribute who I am now to body building.

There was a "Tradition" that I learnt while working at 492 and that was smuggling out things such as milk, bread, and fruit from the mess, this was different to what happened at 3AD, things had changed over the years and food was not to leave the mess, but the guys from GEMS seemed to be the only ones who would get away with it.

We would mainly do this for the "Baggers" (married guys who would bring their lunch to work in a bag) who wouldn't go to the mess, but wanted milk for their coffee etc., most of us would try to bring something back and could end up with a reasonable stash.

One of my colleagues was a well-known interservice touch football player, and would represent the RAAF throughout the year playing games around Australia, to me he would always walk around with an air of grandeur because of it. As normal we would have our end of year awards the same as other bases, but we didn't have a F.I.G.J.A.M (F..K I'm Good Just Ask Me) award, I suggested that we have an inaugural award for this year's presentations and present it to "Obie" the football player; this was met with complete agreeance. He couldn't believe it when his name was called out to accept the award and asked who came up with this, he was told Chucky (a derivative of Chuckles) and couldn't believe it, he didn't think I had the fortitude to suggest it.

Volley ball was the main lunchtime activity here and many would rally around the court that had been established next to the main hangar. There were a few main characters that would try to take the lime light known as "sharks", these guys would come from anywhere on court to steal a shot away from another player, making a spectacle of themselves in the process, good on you guys, and this was great fun. Furthermore once a week or fortnight, I don't recall exactly, we were granted time on a Wednesday, known as a "sporty" to play volley ball or other sports such as table tennis or gym, from 3pm. We also had an afternoon allocated monthly, if the work load allowed, to play an off base sport such as ten pin bowling or similar, this being my chosen sport.

Another of my interests at the time was inter-service shooting; this would be carried out on a weekend at the Murray Bridge training area. The service rifle at the time was an SLR the same that was used when I went through rookies. As a member of the RAAF shooting team, along with approximately 7 other guys I would take part in the monthly medal shoot held on the 4th Sunday of each month. We would arrive at the base early in the morning to sign out our weapons from the armoury and travel down in a mini bus.

As far as I can remember we all, at least the shooting team, had our own weapons as the base had a relatively small number of personnel and held enough rifles for all to have one assigned to them, this gave us the opportunity to get used to the same rifle and not have to resight every time we went on a shoot. This was a 300 metre range set on a series of mounds, (small hill like structures) which were around 3 metres high, where we would do what was known as a walk down shoot, starting at the 300 metre mound, this is where we would fire our practice and sighting rounds before the scoring shots were fired. The shooters would consist of Army, Navy, Air Force and sometimes Police with the largest number being Army personnel.

There would be a series of untimed, timed and rapid fire serials as we moved down range, these would be carried out in the prone, kneeling, sitting and standing positions all of these positions to be unsupported, with 5 rounds to be fired in each position.

The exact amount of ammunition was to be distributed to the firing party about to commence their walk down, this being four magazines with one not completely full.

Before the start a line would be formed according to what lane the shooter had been assigned, the line was to be kept at all times.

The first scoring shots were from the 300 metre mound where we would fire from all positions except standing. Once everyone had finished that serial we would move down to the 200 metre mound, then onto the 100 metre mound and finally the 25 metre line.

As we would wear hearing protection mainly ear muffs, every sound was muffled other than the sound of your heart beat, which was increasing through the anticipation of the next order, as well as keeping track of the rounds you had fired so you knew when to change magazines.

One of the serials would commence when we were approximately 20 meters from the mound, this was purposeful due to the nature of this particular serial.

We would be given the order for the serial to commence, then, instant panic as everyone would run up the mound to get in position before the order to fire was given.

With hearts racing and out of breath, the order to fire was given; I think this was a watch and shoot serial.

The targets were made of a plastic corflute type of material and depicted either a man in a crouching position or a man charging, these would be deployed depending on the distance the shooter was shooting from. All targets had scoring rings printed on them positioned in the centre mass of the target, clearly visible from all distances. I would always look forward to these shoots, quite an adrenaline rush.

At one point in time I, along with some other members of the team, was able to attend a shoot held in Canberra at RAAF Base Fairbairn; this was a trophy match, although the name of the trophy escapes me. This was contested as usual by Army, Navy and Air force; the police may have been there as well. We travelled over in a Hiace van, the trip taking around two days. The rifle bolts were locked in a separate container, and at any time we stopped for lunch or a rest break someone would stay in the vehicle to safe guard the weapons. Being more or less the halfway point we stayed at RAAF Base Wagga overnight and were accommodated in what used to be the female cells, now transit quarters, situated above the guard house.

One of the guys in the team had a contact at Kapooka Army Recruit Training Base near RAAF Base Wagga, who had organised for us to test out the Defence Forces latest rifle being the F88 Austeyr.

The Army took delivery of these ahead of the Air Force, we were to take delivery sometime after. We were run through the safety brief and using their 25 metre range put a few rounds down range. These weapons used an optical sight with a slight magnification which took little time to adjust to, also very light compared to the SLR due to their plastic body.

F88 Austeyr

The match we were participating in used a similar format to the monthly medal shoot that we were used to.

While there, we were invited to a "303" shoot using some of the hosting RAAF members personally owned WW1 and WW11 303's, using reloaded ammunition, from what I understand due to the fact that new bullets were hard to come by and expensive.

This was my first time firing a 303 at a shooting range; these were a single shot bolt action rifle with a five or ten round clip, not sure which, being reasonably heavy and with nasty recoil as well as open sights, these took a bit of adjusting to.

I managed to be awarded a red cloth badge with crossed rifles that was embroidered with gold metal thread for placing in the top 10.

The cloth badge I was awarded (Unfortunately the red faded to blue)

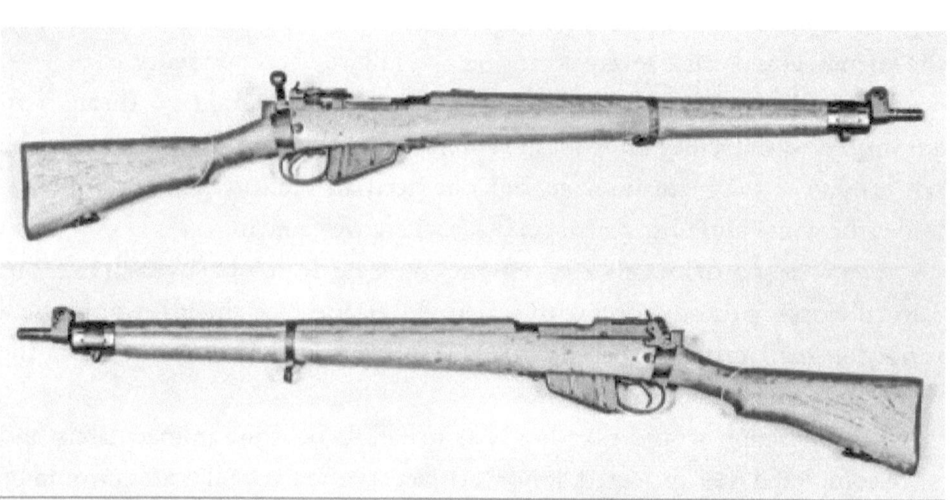

Lee Enfield 303 Rifle

At the end of the main competition the RAAF team won and took the trophy, it was to be retained at RAAF Base Fairbairn.

RAAF Shooting Team with the trophy.

One of our "duties" out of our normal line of work was "Aircraft wash"; this entailed hand washing the P3 Orion's after they had carried out operations over the sea.

These planes would fly low enough to encounter sea spray which, if left on the aircraft, could cause severe corrosion and failure of components.

When the Orion's had landed after a sortie they would go through an automated wash facility known as the "bird bath", this would wash most of the salt residue of the main fuselage, but not from all the intricate area's such as under the wings and undercarriage, that's where we came in.

A crew of approximately 20 personnel, wearing disposable overalls over our normal working dress, along with sealed gloves and face shields, would use a variety of small scrubbing brushes to get into every nook and cranny under the wings and under carriage.

This operation would take hours as it had to be done immaculately and once completed was inspected, if not satisfactory the particular areas would be done again.

This was carried out all year round on a rotation basis, equating to approximately one week of duty per year, where at times it could be freezing cold or stinking hot, none the less it had to be done.

Another duty the more junior ranks had the pleasure of doing, was to organise the morning smoko orders from the canteen, this was a sort of Russian roulette of who was to answer the phone when phoning in the orders, the nice or cranky.

If you were unlucky enough to talk to the cranky one and made a mistake with the order expect some sharp words in reply, everyone who had this job was nervous when phoning the order through.

The same was to be expected when picking up the order, especially if you had to add something on or didn't have the correct money look out e.g. (in a snappy voice) "oh my god couldn't you have included that in the original order", who would think picking up an order could be so stressful.

Rotating to my next section this being AAS (Aircraft Arresting Systems), here the two systems used to stop an aircraft in an emergency landing were maintained and overhauled, as well as keeping them in an operational state ready for deployment when such an emergency arose.

All RAAF bases have AAS, whether military or shared civilian airstrips, only RAAF dedicated strips have both of the following systems, while civilian strips only have Arresting Cables, situated at either end of the main runway to allow for aborted take offs or emergency landings:

The two systems are identified as 1). Arresting net or barrier, 2). Arresting cable.

The net is only to be used for aircraft that aren't propeller driven and can also be used as a back up to the arresting cable.

Fighter jets are the only aircraft capable of using the arrestor cable; they have a hook that is hydraulically deployed by the pilot, which in turn hooks onto the cable.

Both of these systems were collectively known as "Barrier systems" hence the members who maintained them were known as "Barrier crew".

On most bases this was carried out as a duty, and the "Barrier crew" would be a rostered position alongside our normal job on a seven day basis, fortunately at RAAF Edinburgh it was a more permanent crew where "Barrier" was our normal job, as well as carrying out scheduled overhauls of barrier systems from other units around Australia, along with spare systems used as swap over's.

The crew could be called upon at any time day or night to repair any system or be called out for an emergency landing, therefore being on standby for the duration that flying was on.

If the crew were to go to lunch at the mess we would go as a team in the barrier vehicle, and take a hand held radio with us in case there was an emergency while at lunch.

Every morning before flying was to commence the barrier crew would have to carry out "morning services", this entailed communicating with the control tower to enter the barrier site, and to have them operate which ever barrier was being inspected at the time, this was to ensure it was working as expected and to fix any anomalies if needed, while there, all pressures and heights of nets etc. where checked and adjusted if needed.

In the event of a cable arrest, the first thing was to deploy personnel at each side of the cable installation; the next was to have a member go under the aircraft to "unhook" the cable from the hook if it hadn't come out on its own, if the aircraft was still mobile it would be sent off to the flight line, otherwise the runway was closed to other aircraft until it was removed.

Meanwhile the crews on either side were preparing to rewind and make ready the cable as quickly as possible. This was done using a petrol engine rewind unit that is part and parcel of the arresting cable. Depending on the base some of the units were above ground and others underground, and all commands were carried out using hand signals.

The cables were bought back into position evenly and reset ready for the next arrest.

This procedure would be practiced when time and a lull in aircraft movement allowed, as well as qualifying a new or overhauled installation, pilots would also have to engage the cable yearly as part of their emergency procedures qualification.

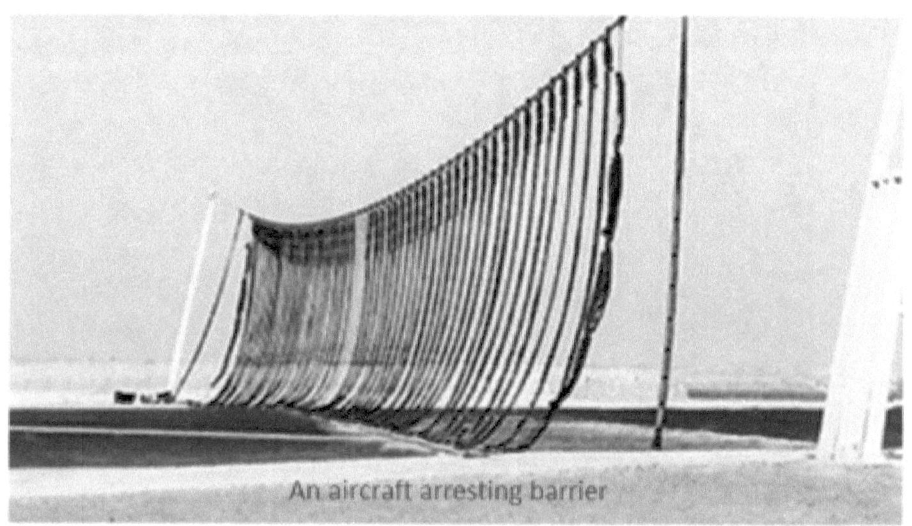

Aircraft arresting cable down Aircraft arresting cable up

F18 Hornet with hook deployed

Whenever travelling on the airfield certain protocols would have to be adhered to, such as seeking permission from the control tower via radio whenever crossing runways or taxiways, as well as entering the barrier site.

This entailed correct radio procedures and to be quick and precise with any communication, it just so happened one of the guys that was in the crew was a chatter box, and would purposefully make a lot of noise when I was in charge of the radio.

Before a request is made over the radio you have to be clear in your mind what you are going to say, something I found very hard to do when someone is very vocal leading up to a request.

Sure he would shut up when I started to ask for permission to cross the runway or enter somewhere, but sometimes the words would come out incorrect, or I would forget what I was about to say.

He thought this was a great joke and everyone else would play along with him, I was always on the lookout on how to get back at him.

The day came along when I found a way to repay his shenanigans. One day this guy (Sando) was loading some gear into the barrier truck and then went off to get more, the workshop was empty at the time except for me whom he hadn't spotted, so I would take the items he loaded into the truck back out and put them on the floor.

I kept out of sight and just watched him when he returned; he looked very disturbed and scratched his head, putting the things back into the truck.

I did this a second time when he went off for more supplies and on his return the same actions, he couldn't work it out, I'm sure he thought he was going mad, then he drove out and until this day he never found out what happened, you may think a hollow victory, but for me, got ya.

There is a variety of support equipment used on the base; these were known a "GSE" or Ground Support Equipment, the section that maintained this equipment was surprisingly named "GSE". Comprising of mainly specialist equipment built for purpose, this included; generator sets, air-conditioning units, bomb loaders, to name a few, this was to be my next internal move.

All the equipment was on a scheduled maintenance regime, and it was our responsibility to bring it in from the flight line when required for service.

There were multiple pieces of equipment available to the end users, and if something that required servicing was is in use we would exchange it with another of the same if available, otherwise we would come back at a later time.

My section had at its disposal a tow motor (similar to what is seen in use at airports for moving baggage trolleys around) that was used to hook up and bring in, and after return pieces of equipment when needed.

The majority of equipment was mounted to a four wheel platform with the front axle being articulated, in other words had an independent steering system.

Where most towable trailers encountered in civilian life, have a draw bar fixed to the frame and pivot on the tow hitch of the towing vehicle to manoeuvre, these would have to be steered into position when reversing into a work bay making reversing an art.

One would have to take into consideration which way the steering mechanism was going to direct the trailer in respect to the angle of the draw bar, and where the tow motor was going to end up, for some this took many attempts and some would give up, unhitch the trailer, turn the tow motor around and use the hitch at the front of the tow motor, a practice that was often laughed at.

Yes this was a pain, something I managed to master at an early stage, but I guess a necessary evil which allowed for precise positioning near aircraft if needed, not that the aircraft tech's using them would worry about that and would seldom reverse them.

When someone carried out a tricky reverse manoeuvre in one attempt, they would normally receive accolades from onlookers watching in awe.

Another strange piece of equipment was our bomb loaders, these were self-propelled and had rear steer, where the driver sat just behind the rear wheels, and the bombs would be over the front wheels when loading an aircraft.

The rear steer made them very manoeuvrable, but because the steering was at the rear wheels the back of the loader would move dramatically left to right.

The loaders had a 4 speed manual transmission, but wouldn't travel any more than 40 kph or so thankfully as they were very unstable even at low speed, after all they were primarily a bomb loader not a form of transport, but we were always up for a challenge, and the challenge was to drive them as fast as they could go, changing up through the gears and trying to keep them in a straight line, not as easy as it may seem.

I recall a situation where one of the guys I worked with hadn't driven one before, and thought it was going to be simple, so he asked if he could return one to the armament section at the back of the base after it had been serviced, so I agreed and followed him up in the tow motor knowing it was going to be hilarious.

I informed him of the challenge and he agreed we travelled on some back roads that were scarcely used just in case and thankfully there wasn't anyone using them.

All I could do was burst into laughter all the way, as I watched him weave from one side of the road to the other hearing him cry out "Whoa" every time as he tried to keep control of the bomb loader, when we arrived at our destination I couldn't stop laughing and he was shaking like a leaf, he said to me I don't know how you guys do it.

At one stage I witnessed a flight line tech crash one of these into a building.

I was testing a cherry picker at the back of the hangar, and had taken it up to its full extension where I had an interrupted view of the whole area. I spotted this guy taking a bomb loader from its allocated parking position, thinking, this could be interesting, sure enough being a bit too cocky as some of the aircraft techs are, he took off flat-out and immediately lost control swinging it into a small storage shed and rammed into the wall putting a large hole into it, I guess he would have had some explaining to do and be a little more careful in the future.

An MJ1 Bomb Loader

Another challenge we came up with was when testing the boom of a cherry picker. It had to be raised by the person in the basket to full extension, and the basket had to be rotated until it was almost tipping out the person operating it, this is at a height of approximately 15-20 metres off the ground.

This was crazy and not a part of the required testing procedures, none the less it's amazing what peer pressure can achieve, from memory I don't think we used safety harnesses.

It was surprising how windy it could get at that height, some guys would freeze due to the pucker (scare) factor, but thankfully the main drive unit had the facility to switch from boom control to ground control allowing the boom to be lowered by someone watching on, enabling the operator to get out.

At some stage safety practices were revised, that stopped all the fun times, where it became mandatory to wear safety harnesses before any operation of a cherry picker, including taking it from point A to point B, what a pain in the arse.

"The Trolley of Death"

While I'm on the subject of "fun times" this brings to mind a tradition among the lower ranks at 492 SQN GEMS, and that was known as the "Trolley of Death".

This was bought out on your birthday; basically a flatbed trailer was used to tie the normally reluctant participant down, spread eagle on their back.

Prior to this happening the "birthday boy" would be found and surrounded anywhere, any time, some would make a run for it, some would react violently throwing punches, some of the big guys would be really challenging, but no one escaped.

I didn't resist too much when my time came around, as I saw it as useless and possibly more injuries.

A broom stick would be put through the sleeves and across the back of your overalls and zipped tied in place along with zip ties around the ankles of your overalls, then you would be tied to the trolley, at least the perpetrators would either put goggles or a face shield on to protect your eyes.

Then a concoction of all manner of oil, grease, food colouring and whatever they could lay their hands on was poured on your chest, then your overalls were zipped up to your neck and the fire hose was stuck up your trouser leg, filling up and squirting water out everywhere.

That was the first step, now you were towed around all the sections, which could be a fair distance away from where it all started, and have more gunk thrown at you, this being on a trailer that had no suspension and going over some rough terrain, this could take 10 to 15 minutes before you would return and be released.

This being condoned by the higher ranks seen as "Moral Boosting", not all would participate, but you would make sure when the time came, to return the favour with the ones that did.

I learnt not to mention anything about my upcoming birthday, and managed to get by on several occasions, this practice was banned a couple of years later due to laws being past, stopping this sort of behaviour and possible law suits ensuing, do you think I, along with everyone else was happy about that, hell yes.

The way we carried out our work compared to how work was carried out on the other side of the road, being the "Aircraft Technicians", was vastly different mainly due to the mere fact that aircraft were airborne and a little more "high tech" than any of our equipment, everything was done "open book" to the letter regardless how many times a particular procedure had been carried out, where we on the other hand only referred to a manual occasionally.

To give us a taste of how things were done in the Aircraft world, we were given the opportunity to carry out a role in the "Wheel Bay" for a 3 month period; here we would work with a Corporal Airframe Technician aka "framey".

It doesn't sound like much, but a bit more involved than changing tires on a truck or car.

Every morning there would be a trolley or trolley's waiting with main and nose wheels from P3 Orion's, that had been changed during the night shift, every main assembly of an aircraft had serial numbers including the wheels and tires, this would be updated on the data base whenever there was a change, and this was particular to each aircraft.

The tires would be re-treaded a certain amount of times before they were scraped, that would be tracked on the data base, we always had a predetermined number of wheel assemblies on hand.

The wheels were of a two piece construction, the main wheels with at least 50 bolts and the nose approximately 20, it took both of us to disassemble and assemble a wheel, with one on each side, and the main wheels were so big we couldn't see each other.

We used a predetermined sequence to know which bolt was to be loosened or tightened, one had a spanner the other a rattle gun and we would move from one bolt to the next instinctively, removing the bolts as we went and the opposite when we were assembling the wheel, barely tightening the bolts initially, then the same operation only this time with a torque wrench, tightening the bolt to specifications. The wheel bearings would be cleaned and inspected then repacked with grease, and stored ready to go, and the bolts were cleaned then sent to NDI (Non Destructive Inspection), where they would pass and be reused or fail and be thrown out.

Nitrogen was used to inflate the tires and this was supplied in large pressurised bottles, the inflation process was carried out in a large metal cage, where up to 4 main wheels or nose wheels would be inflated simultaneously, to a pressure of something like 220psi and 120psi respectively, once the wheels were connected to the inflation hoses, the cage was shut and the airman carrying out the procedure would sit in a chair well away from the cage, and using a "Deadman's" switch (a puenamic switch that would cut off the supply of nitrogen if let go) would hold it down until the tires were inflated to the required pressure, as the tires seated onto the sealing bead of the rim, they would do so with a loud bang and scare the hell out of you.

Prior to the Deadman's switch, from what I gather, the regulator on the nitrogen bottle was relied on to control the supply of nitrogen, this could be set incorrectly and have a tire explode due to over inflation, and the bottles were capable of supplying 2200 psi.

These radical safety precautions were bought about due to accidental over inflations, causing explosions and injury to personnel, there were safety posters in the wheel bay and surrounds, with graphic reminders of what could happen if these precautions were ignored.

Anyway a slight change of topic, but still in the wheel bay; a strange way to welcome me into the section was when the flight line guys more or less ganged up on me soon after I started in the wheel bay.

Someone had put a message on the white board for me to ring Sue Ridge at the water board along with a number, so I did without realising the connection, unknown to me it was the number of the sewerage treatment works, and the person on the other end of the line informs me that there is no one with that name there, and suggests someone is playing a trick on me.

Immediately as that happened people come from everywhere laughing their heads off, how small can a person feel, good one, smart arses.

The wheel bay was known for its "special" wall paper; nearly every square inch was adorned by pinup girls making it unique to the squadron, there was a culture of soft and hard core pornography throughout the Defence Force, where magazines such as these were available in most common areas.

Soon after arriving in the wheel bay directives were handed down banning all forms of demeaning literature across all forces, brought on by the realisation of sexual harassment, with this the wheel bay was transformed back to a normal workshop with nothing adorning its walls, the end of an era.

With that experience behind me it was back to GEMS and working at "Tanker" section, this was positioned away from the main maintenance facilities, more on the outskirts of the airfield due to the size and nature of the equipment being maintained, this being fuel tankers and runway sweepers, also closer to the airfield for easy access to the bulk fuel installation and a larger compound to facilitate the fleet of trucks, where the drivers would also be stationed.

This was a different challenge where most work was heavy, and my first experience working on fuel equipment at this level.

Most of the Tankers were semi-trailers, meaning the trucks were coupled to a 30,000 litre fuel tanker by means of what is known as a fifth wheel allowing connection and disconnection of the truck trailer unit, other tankers were a fixed chassis, but of a lesser fuel carrying capacity.

The trucks were straight forward enough, but the tankers were a mystery unto themselves, as all the valves and actuators needed for their operation, were operated by pneumatics and the tankers were capable of both refuelling and defueling aircraft (defueling or removing fuel from an aircraft would be carried out prior to maintenance) although there would be a dedicated defuel tanker to minimise the risk of fuel contamination with the main fuel storage tanks.

The pneumatics were a very complex system that could take hours to diagnose if something malfunctioned.

This along with "high level sensors" that were designed to shut off individual compartments in the tanker of which there were 4, as they reached maximum capacity. These were mainly used for emergency shut off, as it was a practice to visually gauge the fuel level in each compartment in case the sensors failed and caused a fuel spill, this wasn't acceptable as it could seep into the ground water causing contamination.

Most of the aircraft would run on Aviation Turbine fuel or AVTUR, but some smaller aircraft would use Aviation Gasoline or AVGAS.

AVGAS was compatible with car engines and when available, a few of us would pump some into our cars from the fuel drums we used to discarded fuel in, after draining filter housings etc., this worked better if mixed 50/50 with normal petrol. I found this very beneficial seeing my car was a thirsty V8.

This was seen as a bit shady, but having said that most who worked at Tankers would use it. AVTUR was not used so much, it is similar to diesel fuel and has been known to work ok for some although is seen a little more risky.

While working in tankers I also carried out a "fuel quality control" course, this gave me the credentials to maintain the components of the fuel farm such as the main filter housings, which had scheduled filter changes throughout the year, along with fuel testing.

The other trucks as I have mentioned earlier were runway sweepers, the sweepers use a rotating brush and vacuum unit powered by a separate v8

Cummins diesel engine inside the sweeper, comprising a number of large bags configured vertically that would capture any dirt, rocks etc. from the runway.

The truck was also configurable for wet as well as dry use. After any operation the sweeper would be taken to an appropriate area and through a hydraulic vibration unit, the bags would be vibrated to dislodge any material captured through the sweeping process and dumped on site.

Due to the bags not being able to release all the dirt, they would periodically have to be removed and sent away to be dry cleaned, this job was the least liked by anyone, as there was barely enough room for a person to fit in amongst the bags, and only a small hatch on the side of the sweeper housing to gain access to the encloser, the dust was so fine it would find its way into everything and anything regardless how well it was sealed.

In summer we could only stand to be inside the sweeper for no more than 10 to 15 minutes at a time, due to the cramped conditions and the heat, two of us would alternate to allow for recovery.

It was impossible to use any sort of cooling fan because of the fine dust, and the only light we had was from a lead light we would take with us.

This truly was a shit job, one I really hated along with everyone that had to endure it. The sweepers were to be updated to bagless unit's years later, thank god for that.

Ford Ebling 1313 Runway Sweeper

While in Tanker section I was given the opportunity to carry out a role as a fuel tanker driver on Exercise Pitch Black 1993 in Darwin.

The personnel participating as tanker drivers in the exercise had to complete a tanker driver's course, along with a runway sweeper course prior to the exercise commencing, this taught us everything from filling a refuelling tanker, to the correct way of driving to and approaching an aircraft parked on the holding area, both with the aircraft running (hot fill) and stationary, as well as using all the different types of refuelling trucks.

We learnt the procedure of rolling out the hoses and connecting them to the aircraft, along with the earthing of the tanker and aircraft to the ground, (this is to dissipate static electricity caused by the movement of the fuel in the tanker and while fuel is being dispensed) as well as the paperwork needed each time a delivery is carried out.

This was a crash course and I was glad to get it over and done with.

Then there was the runway sweeper course; this is generally carried out late at night after all aircraft movement has ceased, therefore this was a sleeping duty with accommodation in a small building near tanker section.

This would be carried out at either end of the runway due to rubbish being brought onto the strip from the momentum of aircraft landing or departing close to the edge.

This had to be slow and methodical so as not to miss anything that could be sucked into any aircraft engines intake, the only lighting was supplied by floodlights on the sweeper. Being a very boring job, I was hoping I wouldn't have to do it very often.

Once we arrived in Darwin we were housed in the on base temporary accommodation, along with the other members attached to the exercise and this area was known as "tent city", although the majority of accommodation was in transportable huts; this was a more substantial type of building, with 2 to a room and shared ablutions.

Due to my inexperience in refuelling aircraft, the powers to be thought my services would be put to better use working with the Singapore Air Force, who were also participating in the exercise with F-16 fighters and A-4 Skyhawk's, they were positioned away from the main operational area, and had their own Headquarters and accommodation already setup, more or less a permanent fixture as they visited Darwin on a 12 monthly schedule, to enable them to use our airspace for training purposes.

They would use an in ground (Hydrant) refuelling system, whereby plumbing coming directly from the fuel installation would allow a certain type of refuelling truck to connect directly to it, and in turn refuel their aircraft.

The trucks were known as "Pie Carts", due to their resemblance to a small vehicle used for the supply of pies etc. or more accurately "Hydrant Carts".

The "Pie Carts" used a system where in the event a hose was dislodged from its stowed position when travelling along the road, the brakes would automatically be applied preventing undue damage to the hose and other components.

The only problem with this was that just going over a bump could cause a hose to move enough for this to happen and without warning; the driver would find himself potentially going through the windscreen.

There was a big over ride button on the dash that would release the brakes; some drivers would travel with this depressed although not the smartest idea.

I remember having to travel over some unsealed terrain approaching the Singaporean outpost and having this happen; luckily I was ready for it and was travelling slowly, none the less I still nearly face planted the windscreen.

The Singaporean airman would be waiting for me as I arrived, and would start unreeling the hoses and earth cables before I even had the chance to get out of the truck, this made my job super easy, the only problem with this was at times they would connect the earth cables in the wrong order, as there was a procedure on how everything was connected (truck, aircraft, hoses) and in doing so a spark could jump as a clamp was being connected to its earthing point, due to the possibility of static electricity being presence, not a good idea when fuel vapours are around.

I learnt that I had to be quick enough to stop that from happening and mostly I was.

The USAF (United States Airforce) were also participating in the exercise and among other aircraft they had two B52 bombers in their line-up, apparently RAAF Darwin is the only airfield in Australia able to accommodate them due to their enormous wing span, where the tips of the wings are supported by jockey wheels.

They were parked on a section of the operational area that also had hydrant points, as refueling with a refuelling truck would take too long.

It took hours to fill up these guys, this was also true of their mid-air refuelers, being KC-135's, I remember having to sit holding onto a Deadman's switch (a small hand held unit that shuts off fuel delivery if it is let go) while refueling one, where my shift finished and another driver came along to continue with the operation.

This was my first major exercise and it was a blast, also my first experience working at RAAF Darwin so different to anywhere else.

Two B52 bombers off to the left, pie cart in foreground

KC – 135 mid-air Refueller

Back at 492SQN after the exercise and working at "Heavy vehicle" section, this is where vehicles such as aircraft tow motors, heavy duty forklifts, trucks, cranes, backhoes, buses and mobile truck mounted work platforms were maintained and repaired, it was also around this time my mustering underwent a name change from MTFITT to GSEFITT (Motor Transport Fitter to Ground Support Equipment Fitter), this didn't change anything about the job only broadening the job description.

It was also around this time that the RAAF finally received its supply of F88 STEYR rifles, to replace their aging SLR's in 1996; consequently over the next few month's everyone underwent conversion training, along with a complete revision of associated rifle drill.

During my posting at RAAF Edinburgh there was an attempt to get a precision drill team under way; I was interested and turned up to the first meeting.

To ascertain where everyone sat as far as general marching skills were concerned, we were formed up and were given some basic commands, one being about turn and it became quite apparent then that some were a little rusty, some turned to the left and some turned to the right, the correct movement was to the right, the instructor realised he had some work to do before we got into the fancy routines.

This was an initiative of one of the 1RTU (NO1 Recruit Training Unit) instructors and not an official RAAF directive; therefore it was to be carried out after hours, and unfortunately due to this the numbers dwindled after a while, and consequently the idea was scrapped.

A few months later I was informed that I was to be posted to Darwin, I was in a relationship at the time and a decision would have to be made whether my girlfriend would like to join me on the posting, she said she would like to.

I took it to the next level and asked her to marry me, she said yes, soon after that we were married at the registry office, this entitled us to all the benefits a married couple could access such as; full removals, travelling allowances, motel accommodation on arrival while arranging a married quarters.

From memory we were given 8 days to make the journey by car, but I think we managed to do the trip in 5, giving us a few days to relax before I started work.

Our furniture was to be put in storage in Adelaide while posted to Darwin, and we would pick furnishings from a central furniture store managed by the department of defence, from memory this was for economic reasons due to the distance Darwin was from any other base, my effective date being 17JUL96.

So another send off and plaque to commemorate my time at RAAF Edinburgh, a very pleasing posting where I gained a great deal of experience, and made lots of friends due to my extended time there.

492 SQN "Presento"

Chapter 6
RAAF Darwin

RAAF DARWIN SHARED the runway with the civilian airport on the other side of the strip; this wasn't unusual as a few bases around Australia also had this arrangement.

I was posted to MEOMS (Mechanical Equipment Operations and Maintenance Section) at 321 ABW (Air Base Wing), my first position was with "Tankers" or "FEMS" (Fuel Equipment Maintenance Section), working with the same equipment that was at 492 SQN, the only difference being the constant heat and working basically in a tin shed, this took a bit of getting used to.

Darwin's weather was divided into two seasons, wet and dry. During the wet season, starting in December, the humidity was unbearable at times, and you could set your clock by the storms coming through every afternoon around 4.00pm.

They were so intense that the monsoon drains alongside the roads on base were like raging rivers, but leading up to the wet was the "build up", otherwise known as the "silly season", where the humidity was so dramatic at the end of the day, it felt as if the heavens were going to open up, even the cloud formations said as much, then it all dissipated.

This would drive some people mad or "silly", I found this really hard to handle, but what could I do, everyone had to live with it.

If you were near the airfield you could witness the clouds rolling in then disappear as the immense heat coming off the runway would evaporate them.

The dry was reasonably short approximately 2 - 3 months, even so everyone was looking forward to it for some relief, this was around mid-year, it was still hot, but without the humidity, every day would be around 32 degrees Celsius, cooling down to possibly 17 of an evening.

Due to the constant heat in the Northern Territory, we all had to be vigilant about exposure to the sun, taking all the precautions needed to combat it.

This is not uncommon for all of Australia, but there are some peculiarities in the tropics and one that comes to mind is something I will try to describe.

I remember someone at 492SQN giving me some advice before I left for Darwin, he said to "look out for crotch rot".

You might say "What" but, this apparently is due to the constant heat and humidity we, meaning men, endure around our crotch area, because it doesn't have much of a chance to air out, as it were, and the skin between our legs would, want for a better word, "rot ".

Initially I hadn't notice anything out of the norm and really didn't give it a second thought, then, sometime later, I noticed a strange smell that seemed to be coming from me when I was getting changed, and thought this warrants some investigation.

Upon looking into it, there it was, oh what a sight, a manky mess of skin on the inner crotch area of my legs, I don't recall it being painful at the time, just unsightly.

As soon as I could, I paid a visit to Medical Section, who verified that it was indeed what I thought it was. They gave me an antibacterial cream to remedy it, after a week or two it healed up and I don't think it reoccurred.

One of my colleagues "Vic" thought he had the answer, he didn't wear any underwear, and that was quite apparent when he was working under a vehicle.

We all wore "short" shorts in the tropics; therefore I made it a practice to be out of the line of site when working with him if at all possible.

While in Darwin the RAAF, along with all defence organisations, had recently undergone a restructure, where a large number of positions filled by members in uniform, had been offered redundancies and were replaced with defence civilians, many of which were the same personnel who took redundancies, but under different contracts and pay structure, this was due to budget cuts at the time, this wasn't particularly a good thing.

In a bid to further stop the reduction of members in uniform, there were certain criteria put in place by the Department of Defence that could only be filled by military members, this entailed more robust training such as being "locked on base" for a period of time.

Where personnel would carry out their daily work routine throughout the day, as well as attending lectures on enemy infiltration etc., and then after work move to a "defensive" position near the airstrip to learn and enact the finer details of defending the airbase, such as VCP's (Vehicle Check Points), manning gun pits, and being attacked by "enemy" at 0200 etc.

Our accommodation during this time was in small individual tents or "hootchies" as well as living off ration packs, being upgraded to field kitchens in the following years, oh and another thing, the service provisioned mosquito repellent.

While this sure did the job, it stung like a bastard. This was applied over "camo" paint plastered all over your face; this sure made a mess, especially when mixed with your sweat, and was a cow to remove.

While experiencing the "base lock on" we would be carrying weapons loaded with blanks, and the weapon in the correct state of readiness this normally being the "action" position, that's when a round is in the chamber and the safety is on.

Every now and then spot checks were carried out, to ensure everyone had there weapon in the correct state of readiness; to ascertain this, the rifle would first have to be "cleared".

The first thing that was apparent when clearing a weapon, would be a round ejecting from the chamber, if not this would mean it wasn't in the correct state of readiness, causing trouble for the owner.

Thank god the "lock on" would only occur once a year, we all saw this as a pain in the arse, but necessary.

One of my roles while at Darwin was working as the spare parts procurer, where my job was to order parts and drive all over Darwin picking them up.

Nearly everything was locally sourced with many parts being readily available, as there were a reasonable amount of industrial companies as well as the Army having similar equipment to us, therefore a reasonable support network. If a special order was needed it could take a while to turn up, leaving some equipment sitting out the back waiting for a while.

This was a great job where I met a lot of people, and was able to get away from the base daily.

Around this time, my then wife decided she wanted to leave both me and Darwin; this, unfortunately wasn't an unusual situation on remote bases.

We tried to keep it together for approximately 12 months, but she wasn't happy, it was ok for me because I had my career, but for her life was a struggle.

She returned to Victoria and I had to hand over the married quarters, I decided to live in a privately rented house as I had a dog to look after, rent was not cheap in Darwin, but worth it to have my own space.

We didn't contact each other again until some years down the track when I applied for a divorce.

As promotions were very slow in my mustering, one would have to wait for someone to leave in the higher ranks to allow everyone to progress and for me especially, I had lost all my seniority from my prior enlistment when I re-joined in 1988.

I was finally promoted to Corporal while at RAAF Darwin after 10 years' service from when I reenlisted and received my 15 years long service medal there as well.

CPL slides Long Service medal (front & back)

Every Monday there would be a parade in working dress, carried out at individual sections throughout the base, where everyone was inspected for dress and bearing, this would include haircuts and condition of uniform and part of our uniform was to have name tags sewn in above the right pocket.

It was noted by "Gomer" (so named because his last name was Pywell, "Gomer Pyle" being a well known character in a military comedy in the 60's), the Flight Sergeant carrying out this particular inspection, that there were a few without name tags and to have them sewn on by next week's parade.

That was ok, so I suggested jokingly to the guy's in SPV (Special Purpose Vehicles), where I was working at the time, that we should put name tags all over our uniform next week, they thought that was a great idea, then I thought to myself, oh shit now were in for it.

Anyway previously I had the "equipo's" (the guys who procure such things), order name tags with "Chuck" embroidered on them.

The following week came around and we went over to the main hangar for parade, name tags on hats, shorts as well as our shirts, and I had Chuck on the toe of one boot and Chaffey on the other not knowing what to expect.

As it turned out Gomer wasn't there and consequently someone else took the parade, and as usual had a couple of Sergeants in tow, I think they all saw the funny side.

The next day Flight Sergeant Pywell came to work and heard about our little stunt, unfortunately he didn't see the funny side, and subsequently called a parade to brief everyone in the section on what he thought.

I think he said something about disrespect, and if he was there at the time he would have charged all involved with insubordination, he was "slightly" angry, we all thanked our lucky stars, nothing more come of it.

Name tags

As with other postings there were "rostered duties" involved, and at RAAF Darwin it was guard duty, from memory this was a more or less 24hr sleeping duty carried out on a rotating schedule.

I think there were four personnel per shift.

We would finish work early, go home, have a shower and change into uniform before heading to the guard room to relieve the personnel coming off shift.

We would sign in and organise which position we were to occupy, as two would be in the guard room and two in the guard box managing the boom gate.

The members in the guard room would issue temporary passes mainly for contractors working on base, as well as issuing and receiving keys for the various buildings on base, ensuring the personnel signing for them were authorised.

Meanwhile the members operating the guard box checked the pass or I.D of anyone entering the base; this would also include people on foot and on bicycles, saluting officers and women as a courtesy, raising and lowering the boom for each individual vehicle.

The guard box was air conditioned, but due to the constant opening and closing of the doors when it was raining. The windows would fog up and make it very difficult at times to identify an approaching vehicle.

Some people would try to enter the base without their I.D, especially officers who would state something along the lines of; don't you know who I am, this was usually replied with, sorry sir I can't let you on without your I.D. They would then be turned around or directed to the guard house to fill out a temporary pass, some would get so angry you could nearly see steam coming out of their ears.

Contractors working on the base would also try to enter after their temporary pass had expired, they would also be sent to the guard room.

This was a real pain, especially first thing in the morning when everyone was trying to get to work, only to have these inconsiderate people disrupting the flow.

We would rotate positions throughout the shift and later in the night personnel in the key positions would reduce to just one and the others would try to get some sleep in the quarters provided, something I could never get the hang of.

These duties are a pain, thankfully it wasn't that often.

Every Friday morning at 0630, being cooler before the sun came up, there was a decreed run/walk known as the CO's run, where as many personnel as possible were to attend, other than those that had pivotal roles on base, even though many reasons why some didn't make it, were hard to accept.

This would comprise a 2.4 km run or a 5.8km walk marked out by the PTI's (Physical Training Instructors), sometimes through the married quarters and down to the golf course, or around the perimeter of the base along with other tracks. This was to be completed in a reasonable time and we would make our way back at our leisure, I think we started work around 0900 to allow for cooldown and recovery.

Due to Darwin being classed as a remote location, all personnel were given an allowance equivalent to air travel to the closest major city, in this case Adelaide.

This was to compensate for the remoteness and sometimes boredom of Darwin.

We could also put this towards an overseas trip if we so desired, and seeing that I hadn't travelled out of Australia at this time I decided to visit Bali which is only 2 hours away from Darwin.

My allowance covered airfare, accommodation, 4 or 5 side trips and some meals, just what the doctor ordered.

As the Defence Force was undergoing many changes around this time, all bought on by budget cuts, one such change was the introduction of JLU's (Joint Logistic Units), these units were formed to best utilize the now depleted numbers of members in uniform and to pool resources.

These units would be put under the control of a Commanding Officer chosen from any of the Armed Forces (Army, Navy, and Air force), my unit 321 ABW, was taken over by JLUN (Joint Logistic Unit North), and an Army Commanding Officer.

From what I understood at the time there were 3 other JLU's; JLUEast, JLUWest and JLUSouth created, although my memory and understanding may be wrong, we were promised that this would not fundamentally change anything, but of course it did.

As I have mentioned earlier the RAAF is generally not as military focused as the army, but this was about to change.

Our day to day routine became what the army would recognise as normal, with a regime of sport and PT every morning for 2 or 3 hours among other nuances.

This interfered with our work output dramatically, and questions were being asked at the top regarding the availability of serviceable equipment on the flight line.

This went on for approximately 12 months, with our chain of command fighting for us to return to the control of the RAAF.

This finally got through to the politicians who had brought this on and we returned to RAAF leadership, only to face yet another change of unit this being 321CSS (Combat Support Squadron).

Within the space of 12 months I started at 321ABW, transitioned to JLUN and then to 321CSS without moving an inch, quite ironic, talk about an identity crisis.

While with JLUN, I was managing SPV (Special Purpose Vehicles), as the name implies, vehicles with specific applications such as aircraft tow motors, aircraft loading platforms, cranes etc. along with ordering spares, then with this latest change I was put in charge of MCS (Maintenance Control Section) where all the paperwork for maintenance etc. was originated, then my last position before I was posted out, was back at FEMS managing and ordering spares.

Although some of my positions were with managing, a percentage of my time was still heavily involved with hands on work, this was a great combination as I enjoyed working alongside my colleagues and getting up to mischief with them.

Approximately 18 months prior to being posted out of Darwin, I had met a lovely Filipina who had only been in the country for 3 weeks, and a courtship of sorts ensued.

So to cut a long story short, approximately 3 months later we were married, and I began organising her, along with her young son's immigration, this unfortunately had certain technical problems attached.

One of the problems concerned documents that weren't registered in the Philippines, this in turn generated a refusal of the immigration application, this of course was heart breaking, but fortunately we were able to apply for a bridging visa which gave us time to sort it out.

The other problem was her brother in law, who didn't particularly want us to marry, as he had arranged with a benefactor to marry her in exchange for a business loan, and tried his best to make life difficult for us.

I was talking about him to my work mates at one stage, and "Curti" a guy who doesn't take lightly to people causing problems of this ilk, asked if I would like him to pay a visit to this arsehole, of course I declined.

As soon as we were married we were entitled to a married quarter, and found one on a Navy communication base; HMAS Coonawarra, at this time a lot of facilities such as this had become Tri service and shared across the 3 services, this being approximately 10 minutes from the RAAF base.

My wife also had a daughter who was already in Darwin and living with her grandparents, she was to come and live with us once we found a house.

The house we had chosen was built on reclaimed swamp land and that in itself wasn't a problem, but it was infected with small black ticks that liked to attach themselves to my Doberman.

It was a nightly ritual to check and remove them from him; they got into every fold of skin they could find especially between his toes. Because I checked him daily they didn't seem to get a good hold and I basically scrapped them off.

There was a pool on the navy base we frequented every day, and on one occasion we went down and found no one there, we thought was odd until we jumped in, it was freezing, it must have been in the dry season, when the overnight temperature drops to 17 degrees Celsius being very cold for Darwin and very little humidity, which I guess inhibits the heating of the pool water, we tried to warm up by swimming around, but it didn't work, so no pool for a while, damn.

Another thing around this time of year was when going to bed, we would only have a sheet over us and the fan on, but there would always be a quilt at the end of the bed for quick deployment as the temperature would plummet around 0200 and wake you, so the quilt would be pulled up and back to sleep.

Having owned a few motorbikes while in Darwin the one I remember the most was a 1984 Kawasaki GPZ1100 that I found at the local motorcycle wreckers, it was in reasonable condition and all it needed was a good going over and a paint job.

1984 GPZ1100 prior to paint job and dressed up for Darwin's toy run

GPZ1100 after paint job

As I had spent quite a while transforming this bike to reflect my vision of what it could be, near tragedy struck, after having lunch at home this particular day and returning to work, I was turning left onto the highway just outside the base.

I had stopped between the curb and a semi-trailer who was indicating to go right, but suddenly he started to turn left, very quickly moving over toward me, and before I had a chance to get out of the way I was trapped, I looked behind me and all I could see was his trailer wheels about to run over me, as they were heading for the curb where I was. I managed to jump off the bike as his wheels crushed the front wheel of my bike onto the curb, leaving the bike sitting upright in the same position it was when I was on it.

He didn't stop, maybe he didn't realise what had happened as the bike was in the upright position, especially when looking back through the rear vision mirror, and of course there weren't any witnesses.

I found out what company he worked for by checking the guard house log, and sent them a letter explaining the situation and asking for some sort of compensation.

I was advised by a lawyer doing some volunteer work for legal aid in Darwin, that this was the appropriated avenue to take, they (the company) of course denied any knowledge of it, I didn't follow it up any further as I felt I was banging my head against a brick wall.

I managed to repair the damage, being, from what I can remember, the front wheel, both front brake disc's, front forks and the main frame, the frame being the most difficult part to source.

Soon after that I was to be posted to 381 ECSS (Expeditionary Combat Support Squadron) RAAF Williamtown near Newcastle in NSW approximately 3800km from Darwin, this was good news, as we were looking forward to a new start away from Darwin.

The Darwin crew threw a send-off barbecue, and presented me with a plaque commemorating my time there.

My time at Darwin was memorable to say the least, not only work related, but environment and personal events also.

As we were set off on our trip down to the new base, there was wide spread flooding due to record rainfall at the time, this held us up at Adelaide River, approximately 112km south of Darwin, where we were to wait for quite some time before the river subsided, then we were able to continue on our journey down the Stuart Highway.

We travelled down to Williamtown in our MK111 XJ6 Jaguar.

MK111 XJ6 Jaguar

Flooded Adelaide River

"Presento" from Darwin

Chapter 7

RAAF Base Williamtown

AFTER ARRIVING IN WILLIAMTOWN, we were again, as is normal practice, put up in a fully self-contained hotel room for a short period, while we waited for our personal effects to arrive from Darwin, along with my furniture that was to be taken out of storage in Adelaide, and sent over to our married quarter.

The married quarter was preselected in Darwin before we left; saving a lot of time looking for one once we arrived. My Doberman was being sent down by a pet moving company.

Our married quarter was in a small town named Raymond Terrace approximately 15 minutes from the base, this was positioned in amongst civilian houses rather than a group of defence houses, so as to blend into society and make us feel more comfortable.

This was becoming increasingly the norm, as married patches were being phased out and mainly civilian owned defence houses that were leased to the Defence Force, were dotted all over the areas where there was a defence presence.

There were schools and shops not far from where we were living making life a little easier.

Previously I had completed a Fuel Quality Control Centre Operator course, this enabled me to take the position of NCOIC (Non Commissioned Officer in Charge) of FQC (Fuel Quality Control) and here I was to run the Fuel Farm, carrying out low point drains, testing fuel and maintenance as required.

As I would have to travel to work at certain times of the year when the sun was just coming up over the trees, it would make visibility very difficult due to the glare, and I remember navigating by the white lines on the edge and centre of the road alone.

Most of the time I was riding my motorcycle, and I would feel the wind generated by trucks going in the opposite direction without seeing them, this of course was only when I was travelling east for approximately 10 mins, then I would turn right and travel south for the remainder of my trip thanking my lucky stars I made it in one piece.

Low point drains would have to be carried out before any fuel movement was to occur (this was required for Aviation Turbine fuel or AVTUR); therefore my work started at 0630 every morning.

This procedure was necessary due to the fact that overnight, condensation would form inside all the piping and storage tanks, running down to the lowest points where it would be drained off, so as not to mix with the fuel once it started to circulate in the system.

These points were all over the place, and in some cases at the storage tanks, 6 to 8 litres of water could be drain off.

This procedure was performed almost every day, mainly when there was flying programmed.

In the winter months after overnight rain, I would have to wade through freezing cold water captured in the bundings, these are retaining walls installed around the main storage and holding tanks, designed to contain the contents of the tanks in the case of leaks. The water was drained off by the means of a valve, being located outside the bunding walls, which was manually operated; this took quite a while to drain so no hanging around waiting, and would be closed again later when all the water had drained away.

This was all just part of our job, even if it wasn't particularly enjoyable.

What's the big deal if water is present in the fuel, you may ask, well at the altitude many of the aircraft fly the temperatures are such that any water particle mainly microscopic, can freeze in the fuel effectively creating a blockage in fuel lines resulting in an aircraft crash.

Aviation Gasoline or AVGAS was also used, but not many aircraft ran on this fuel and it doesn't have the same condensation issues as AVTUR.

An example of a bunding half full of water.

There was a variety of tests that would be carried out on the fuel to ensure its quality, some of the time I would have help doing this, but more often than not I was on my own due to the other Corporal who "worked" with me, being committed to interservice sport until he was posted out, and replaced with someone who was interested in carrying out this job.

Even though the bulk of water was removed during the low point drains there could still be moisture present in the fuel, to prevent this from happening a Fuel System Icing Inhibitor (FSII) would be added to the fuel.

One of the tests is to determine that the correct amount of FSII had been added at the suppliers.

Other tests are:

- Specific Gravity
- Flash Point
- Particulate contamination

These tests were carried out on all storage and holding tanks (holding tanks were for storage of fuel waiting to be tested and cleared), as well as all refuelling tankers on a programmed frequency, along with the tankers delivering fuel to our facility, where it was tested per delivery.

Due to condensation forever present between the fuel and the walls of the tanks, mould would appear and consequently have to be cleaned off. Therefore on a programmed schedule the tank in need of cleaning would be emptied into neighbouring tanks and manually cleaned with rags soaked in bleach, this was an enormous job and especially in the summer it would be exhausting.

The tanks are huge and hold up to 3 million litres, a few more personnel would be tasked to help in these circumstances.

There was a week of "lock on" here in the same vein as the one in Darwin where at one stage we had a mock battle in the early hours of the morning, but this was more organised than what I had experienced in Darwin.

Prior to this "battle" we had learnt how to install and implement a hard wired communication system, this was between gun pits and supply lines to simulate a war like scenario, along with the correct terminology and how to implement it correctly; this was a little over our heads but we managed.

At the time we were "attacked" everyone other than the personnel on guard duty was asleep in their hootchies (small tents), the communication system was used to alert everyone and we hurriedly manned our posts.

We started to return fire, when the "enemy" fired on us (using blank ammunition), the idea was for unit commanders, of which I was one, to order Ammo supplies as needed while under fire.

Being quite loud it was hard enough to hear yourself speak, let alone maintain the concentration needed to put an order through, here we would use the phonetic alphabet to spell out our requisition (Alpha, Bravo etc.), meanwhile when waiting for supplies to turn up, the guys were shouting bang bang, when they ran out of bullets, what a crack up.

This must have occurred in winter as I remember it being freezing.

In September 2001, 381 ECSS was deployed to RAAF Base Learmonth, a bare base on the North West coast of Western Australia that shared the Learmonth civilian airport.

There are 4 Expeditionary Combat Support Squadrons in Australia, who rotate on a yearly basis to supply deployments to the various bare bases when needed.

A bare base has all the amenities of an operational base including a shared mess and bunkers for medical and radar instillations.

There are also workshops, refuelling facilities and aircraft shelters, and is normally manned by a skeleton crew, unless there is an exercise being carried out or a deployment such as this.

We were deployed there due to the growing amount of "boat people" illegally entering Australia from the north and west, here we supported two PC3 Orion's patrolling these areas.

On arrival, we attempted to pitch 11' x 11' tents near the mess hall for our sleeping quarters, but had problems staking them down, we were trying to drive the tent pegs into what seemed to be asphalt and being plastic pegs they couldn't penetrate the surface, so we abandoned that idea and set up stretchers in our workshop.

One of the personnel posted there was known to me as we worked together at 492SQN, and he was good enough to loan us a TV.

While there on the 11th of September 2001 one of the guys stayed up late watching TV, and witnessed firsthand, news of the attacks on the twin towers, he, in disbelief, woke all of us up to share the news.

When this news officially reached Australia, the Defence Force was immediately put on high alert, this prompted the need for guards on the gates of RAAF Learmonth, due to the aircraft there being a possible target.

A guard roster was hurriedly organised and we manned the gates, monitoring all vehicles and personnel entering the base, we were later relieved of this duty as civilian guards were organised and put in place.

While at Learmonth I received a phone call from back home regarding some problems with my step daughter, asking if I could try to come back early to help sort things out.

I approached the RAAF Chaplain who was deployed with us, to see if he could help me get home early. He was able to do some talking for me and secured a seat on one of the P3 Orion's that was doing a rotation back to Edinburgh, with a slight deviation to Williamtown were we lived.

There were also some other personnel on the flight needing to return as well for their own reasons.

The aircraft stopped at Williamtown overnight, and while there, a message came through for the guys travelling with me, to return to Learmonth, as the Commanding Officer running the deployment cancelled their return home due to manning requirements. They had to immediately catch a commercial flight back to Perth and make their way back to Learmonth from there.

The deployment was initially to last for 3 months, but I was only there for 1 month and from what I can understand, due to the fact I had put in a discharge application prior to the deployment, the Chaplain pushed the point that I shouldn't have been deployed in the first place, and I imagine that's why I was allowed to stay home.

I had put in for discharge as my 20 years of service was due to come up on the 07 JUL 2002, 20 years being a milestone where I was entitled to a part pension at that stage, when I left the RAAF "again".

I had elected to discharge to a small town on the Gold Coast in Queensland, this being Nerang in the Hinterland about half an hour from Surfers Paradise.

I took my long service leave 3 months prior to my discharge date, this allowed us to rent a house while still in the RAAF and pay the married quarter subsidised rate, while we were looking for a place of our own and to find a suitable job.

When the time came to sign my discharge papers, I was to travel to RAAF Amberley, an hour or so from where I was living, and sign them in front of the Commanding Officer, I also had to hand in my ID at this stage.

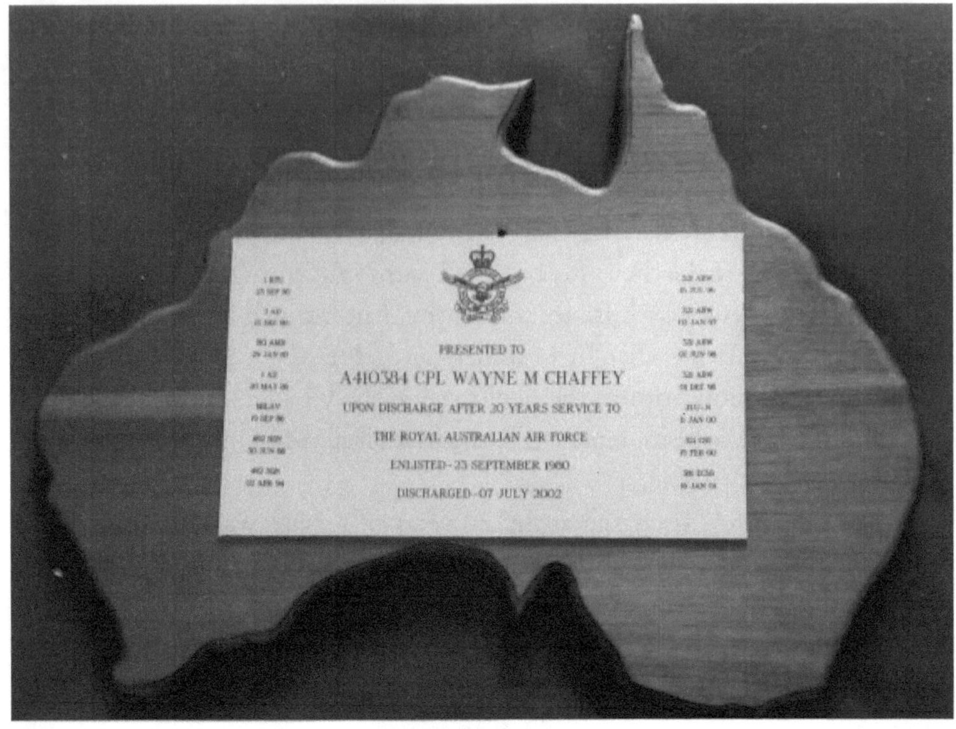

Presento from 381ECSS

Chapter 8
End of 20 years' service

THIS WAS TO BE A NEW chapter in our lives where the RAAF wasn't there to back us up anymore, a chance to be totally independent, well almost.

Prior to leaving the RAAF I had been diagnosed with arthritis in both my knees, where the Defence Force had admitted liability, now was the time to put in a claim to DVA (Department of Veterans Affairs) for recognition, and have them organise compensation.

DVA arranged for a report to be carried out by an Orthopaedic surgeon, basically to outline my complete range of movement, as this was to be a whole of body report.

Upon the outcome of the report, it was deemed my range of movement was within acceptable limits, and my claim was denied.

Now the fun started, I had the right to appeal against this decision, and to do so I needed a second opinion from an Orthopaedic surgeon with higher qualification's than the first, I would also have to pay out of my own pocket for this. If I won the appeal I would have that fee reimbursed.

I managed to find a surgeon who disputed the original outcome and was in my favour, subsequently supplying me with a report to back up my claim.

This sparked off a battle with the Administrative Appeals Tribunal, along with DVA and their bank of lawyers and me on my own.

Well long story short; I won and was awarded a lump sum, not in the realms of what you hear of in civilian cases, none the less a victory, along with a fortnightly payment from DVA, as long as I worked at least 25 hours a week.

This was a very pleasing outcome after a very long drawn out process, especially due to the fact that I had achieved this on my own, without any legal team to back me up, and this being my first experience with anything like this before.

Around this time I had the sad duty of putting my beloved Doberman to sleep as he had developed cancer in the spine, in turn paralysing his rear quarters.

Originally he had a lump on his thigh that developed over the period of a few years; it didn't seem to bother him so I had left it alone, but now, a few more years down the track, I thought it best to get it checked out.

The vet I took him to informed me there was a large spread of cancer, that had travelled to his spine, and that it was necessary for it to be removed. He didn't offer any alternative other than chemo therapy, something that could only be done in Brisbane, and that it was more than likely too far gone to be effective, this seemed like he was clutching at straws and was far too expensive, so I agreed to the surgery.

A few days or so after getting him home, the stiches weren't healing and also paralysis set in, it was devastating to see him drag his hind quarters around, literally tearing the skin off his back legs, and no control over his bodily functions. He would look at me in despair not knowing what was going on.

I wasn't prepared to have him suffer in this way any longer than necessary, so I returned to the vets and had him put to sleep.

I still think to this day that he could have lived years longer if I hadn't done anything, he was 10 years old when he died.

My life changed after that, he made us feel safe as no one would dare enter the property without his approval.

My beloved Doberman "KY"

Finding part time jobs applicable to my qualifications was not easy; the ones I did find ranged from working in a stationary store to dynamically balancing golf clubs.

Only one of them was mechanical to a degree, this being a spare parts interpreter, and that was only a short term position.

Most of the other jobs were temporary other than the golf club position that was around 1 year.

This in and out of jobs got the better of me, when the idea of joining the Air Force Reserves came to mind.

The application for the Reserves was carried out at RAAF Base Amberley, where something I didn't think of come to light.

There is a five year limit from when service personnel leave the service, and then apply to join the reserves, exceeding that time limit meant they would have to suffer rookies again.

I got there just in time, by about 3 months.

As I had an accepted arthritis condition, restrictions were attached to my application e.g. no running or prolonged standing, never the less I was accepted and retained my rank of Corporal.

Something I hadn't realised at the time was that reserve personnel worked in squadrons alongside their PAF (Permanent Air Force) counterparts, in the past reservists had their own agenda and would work in the reserve squadron on obscure projects.

There was a reservist position with 6SQN that was opened up for me, this is a fighter squadron where the then current fighter bombers were stationed, these being F111 aircraft the same ones I took score for while at Evans Head.

6SQN had their own Ground Support Equipment and a small workshop to work out of, and I think 4 GSEFitter's and a General fitter, the boss was a Sergeant with a Corporal and 3 LAC's making up the group.

I was lucky enough to know the Corporal from previous postings and the other guys were very easy to get to know and work with, this was the first operational Squadron I had worked for, all my other postings were maintenance Squadrons.

As a reservist I was obligated to complete 35 or so days a year with the option to apply for more if they were available. As there was a certain number of days budgeted per reserve unit, and seeing I wanted to treat this as a part time job, I was applying regularly for 3 or 4 days a week, and these were approved every time.

Because the base was approximately 1.5 hours away from home I would stay on base for the few nights I was working, I was also entitled to meals while there.

Unfortunately DVA deemed I was earning too much with the reserves and withdrew their payments.

Accommodation while in the reserves was in what used to be transit quarters, primarily for personnel either carrying out courses on base or stopping over briefly, while I was there a new accommodation block was completed just on the outskirts of the base, these were unit style 2 or 3 story buildings and I was able to secure one of rooms, they all had an ensuite with a small kitchenette and a balcony, and each floor had a laundry with washing machines and dryers.

Everyone had under cover parking with a lock up storage room to themselves; this was a sign of the times where the Defence Force finally put a focus on their members and how to retain them.

Breakfast, lunch and dinner was had at the Airmen's mess and because of this I started to pack on some kilo's. The young guys I worked with noticed, and suggested I join them after work in the base gym; I took them up on their offer and soon got back into shape.

Qualifying for weapon handling was one of the things I had to do soon after arriving at 6SQN; this was going to be tough as I hadn't handled a rifle for 5 years, and some of the safety checks had changed due to the age of the rifles, with the possibility of certain parts failing if not carried out in accordance with this.

Prior to the actual test, everyone going through qualifying at the same time as myself, was run through the procedures associated with safety and weapon jams etc., all the elements that will be in the test.

An instant fail if any safety check was missed, well I managed to fail on my first attempt due to a safety breach soon after the test started, after all the years I had been doing this previously, the procedure I knew prior to having the test had become habit and what I had just been shown instantly forgotten, this meant I had to come back at a later stage and try again, this time I got through.

While in the reserves, an opportunity came up to accompany/mentor a group of Cadets associated with the three services (Army, Navy and Air Force), selected from various locations across Australia, on a trip to Darwin.

This was more or less a recruiting drive, I think they were all in their last year of high school; this was to impress them, and possibly persuade some to join a branch of the services when the time was right.

Darwin was chosen because of the close proximity to all three services, we were accommodated on the same Navy base I lived on when I was in Darwin previously.

I found it very interesting that they had access to many operational areas that even serving members wouldn't be able to come close to, e.g. at Robertson

Army Barracks they got close and personal with Abraham tanks, as well as an opportunity to fire some rounds at the Weapons Training Simulation System (WTSS), and with the Navy, HMAS Coonawarra, they all had a ride on one of their Rigid-Hulled Inflatable Boat's (RHIB), as well as having a meal in the officers mess, unfortunately the RAAF didn't have anything as impressive as this to show them.

This was also something I would never have experienced otherwise, equally impressing for me as well as the cadets.

Working at 6SQN was great, with a small number of personnel making up the team, there was enough work to keep us busy all week. Working around the aircraft and being involved with things such as the CO's morning briefing, mixing with the aircraft technicians, understanding mission objectives etc. made me feel part of the action.

I worked here for approximately 1 year and towards the end, because of more budget cuts, reserve hours were to be cut back to the obligatory 35 days or so, some exceptions were made for aircraft trades, but not for mine.

What to do? This was working so well for me, so I decided to apply for the permanent air force again for the 3rd time, it took 6 months to go through due to security checks etc., but I was accepted and I had elected to go to Darwin for the second time.

The situation had changed in the home also and I found myself a single man once more, not much luck on the marriage front for me.

It would seem while absent from home when attending the reserves in Amberley, a door had opened for my wife and the opportunity to find someone new came about, facilitated by her so called friends in the Filipino community, who had introduced her to this home wrecker.

This left me feeling discarded once more, but for some reason slightly expected, as I was away from home more than usual, and she was easily persuaded to go the way of others.

Anyway we sold the house and split the profit and as I had re-joined the RAAF as a married man, I wasn't about to change that just in case the situation turned around.

This also entitled me to a married quarter of which there were plenty available on the base married patch, situated just outside the fence line.

The Defence Force at this time was starting to provide housing in the same way I experienced while at RAAF Williamtown, giving members the opportunity to live next door to civilian households and feel more in touch with the community, the plan was to have all members in homes like this in the not so distant future.

Chapter 9

3rd reenlistment: RAAF Darwin

Here I was in Darwin for the second time, with a start date of 24NOV2008; I started work running the Fuel Equipment Maintenance workshop at 321ECSS.

The workshop had recently been replaced with a new building and in a different location from where it was back in the 90's, so new in fact it was still having minor problems sorted out such as: non-slip floor coating yet to be done properly, and when it was, it was so rough it could take skin off when working under a vehicle.

The smoke detectors were situated incorrectly, where more often than not when a truck started in the workshop it would set fire alarms off; this was due to the extractor fans drawing the exhaust smoke across the detector.

We worked out, that if the circuit breaker for the alarm was temporarily turned off no alarms would be triggered, this of course was not an accepted practice, but was a short term work around.

In the event of an alarm being triggered, fire trucks from the civilian airport would have to respond.

Primarily because RAAF Darwin didn't have their own fire section due to there not being any flying squadrons on base; this was a huge disruption for the civilian Fiery's, every time this happened it would be treated as an emergency, and took one of their trucks and the crew away from the civilian airport.

The smoke sensors were eventually repositioned and no work arounds needed.

Amongst the fuel trucks that we maintained, there would also be some that were leased; these would be maintained by Fleet Management contractors.

The model of runway sweepers that I talked about at 492SQN, had been replaced by a bagless variety, these were driven by hydraulic motors at the wheels and powered by a single diesel engine, making for a more pleasurable maintenance experience.

Most of the jobs carried out in the workshop were organised by the guys on the floor according to priority, job sheets were put in trays that were marked with the current status of each vehicle e.g. service required, waiting on parts, unserviceable (U/S) etc.

There was a relatively new, or new to me computer data base system in place, supposedly to cut down on paperwork, but it produced a hell of a lot more than the system before it, with every service having printouts of all that was required to be done, this was so each item could be initialled by the fitter carrying it out.

Some of the major services would have up to 8 pages of checks/routines to be carried out.

When a job was completed, it was my responsibility to check the paperwork for completion, then it all had to be entered into a data base, it could take a while for each service or U/S to be entered, this would cover the equipment details, the individual time for each technician that worked on the vehicle and all spare parts used.

These job sheets seemed to appear in my in tray on a constant basis, this is where most of my time was spent.

I worked alongside another Corporal who happened to be a colleague I worked with at 492SQN; his main role at the time was sourcing and ordering spare parts.

Due to the new computerised systems taking a great deal of time away from the Corporals on the floor, most positions were filed by two Corporals to enable the office work to be carried out by one, and the supervisory role carried out by the other, there was a stretch of resources at the best of times, this just made it harder.

The two LAC's I had working for me when I first started back at FEMS where a little challenging. As Darwin was more lay back than other bases, some of the personnel were left to their own devices, and when I came along and started to organise things the way I wanted them, I met a little bit of resistance, they were still getting the work out on time, but were used to not having anyone there telling them what to do, this and I think the fact that I had just reenlisted from a reserve position, possibly caused some resentment.

At that stage because of my return to the PAF (Permanent Air Force) after such a long time, I felt a little uneasy when I tried to assert my authority. I needed to rebuild my confidence back up to what it was before I left the service, this improved over time and I gained the respect of the guys working for me, although they still managed to more or less do their own thing.

I also had a defence civilian working for me, he didn't care who I was and had no problems doing what I asked, mainly because his job was more vulnerable than the other guys, the irony of this was, he happened to be the same guy who worked at FEMS when I was at RAAF Williamtown before I discharged, having taken a position here.

Due to everything being monetised in more recent times, certain activities had been scaled down tremendously since I was last in, for instance; there used to be large format CO parades every month, this would be carried out on all bases, where everyone in the squadron would put on their service uniform and form up in flights of let's say 24 men and women, and these flights would make up possibly 5 – 6 hundred personnel being the SQN.

The flights would march individually onto the back of the parade ground forming up at the appropriate position, once all were in position the order would be given to advance and the band or recorded music would start.

On the first note after the second drum roll everyone would step off and March in time to the music towards the dais where the CO was standing. Instead of this a more casual approach had been adopted, where everyone was to attend a gathering at the Airmen's tavern (at RAAF Darwin), and wait for the CO to turn up, sitting or standing at attention when he showed and returning to sitting around as he filled us in on the latest going's on.

Another change was the lack of a "lock on", this had been reduced to 1 day of instruction and everyone went home around 2300.

These measures were bought on by, I would imagine and I may be wrong, politicians ignoring the military importance of these activities, and getting the most out of the reduced personnel. The parades etc. that would normally be carried out throughout the year were costed into a monetary figure, this being taxpayers money "saved" giving the Minister of Defence a pat on the back.

The extra duty to be carried out at Darwin was Barrier crew, and was at times a real time waster.

Because we shared the strip with the civilian airport we would have to wait for a window of opportunity to arise, giving us enough time to enter the barrier site to carry out our checks, this was done the first thing of the morning.

Darwin's airstrip is approximately 3km long and is far from flat, aircraft seem to disappear in certain sections then mysteriously reappear further down, something like a wave in shape with peaks and troughs.

Before we asked permission from Air Traffic Control for anything we would always look in the sky for ourselves, even if there was an aircraft that seemed miles away, we would wait knowing we would be told to hold short (there were designated markers on and around the airfield that we couldn't pass when told to hold short), sometimes we would be lucky enough to have an Air Traffic Controller that would give us permission to cross etc. without us asking, as they would spot us approaching (white vehicle, orange flashing light on the roof and the same time every day), knowing our route and where we were going, this would only happen if they had time to do so.

Our ATC's controlled all air movements happening on and around Darwin Airport, where things could and would get quite busy at times.

There were numerous light aircraft, or "bug smashers" leaving for remote destinations at this time of the morning, taking people to work etc. along with commercial aircraft.

When we did get a window, it might be only for a couple of minutes, we would race in with the vehicle, the guys would run to the barrier doors which opened in an upward direction, as the rewind unit that we checked was underground, but before we went in we started up the extractor fans, we were supposed to check the atmosphere with a "sniffer"(air sampling unit) prior to entering, to ensure the atmosphere was safe, we usually did, but if time was tight we relied on the extractor fans sucking in new air, and still had a sniffer running just in case.

If we needed to vacate the runway in a hurry, due to traffic, (aircraft landing or taking off) and we hadn't finished what we were doing, we would just leave everything as it was, vacate and wait to get back in later. At times we could be out on the airfield for 1 to 2 hours depending on aircraft movements.

Soon after arriving in Darwin I thought I would try to get back into motorcycles, I had stopped riding a few years back due to wrist problems.

I decided to try something with an upright sitting position, my previous bike was a sport bike where the handlebars were orientated in a such a way that I was straining my wrists, I found a dealership that had a demo bike of the configuration I wanted to try, I took it for a ride and I was fine.

With this knowledge I went looking to see what was around and ended up buying a new Suzuki DR650.

Later on I decided to upgrade, and found a second hand Triumph Speed Triple in Melbourne that I had shipped up to Darwin. This was a beautiful bike, but after a while I found even though it had a more or less upright seating position, my wrists would complain due to the handlebar configuration and unfortunately it had to go. I ended up trading it in on a new Triumph Thunderbird that was in the showroom of the local Triumph dealers. I hadn't ridden a cruiser before so this was a new experience; I kept this one for quite a while.

One of the must do's I had planned for Darwin was to buy a track car, as the local motor racing complex was only a short distance from the base – Hidden Valley Motorsport Complex.

I was looking around to see what was available, when one of the civilian motor mechanics working with us, told me he knew of a Toyota Celica previously used in a junior racing category that may be available, he did some digging for me and it turned out it was sitting around not being used, and the owner would be willing to sell it.

I went to check it out and it was just what I was looking for, actually more than I expected, it was fully kitted out for racing, I paid for it straight away and brought it home that day on his car trailer. A little later I built my own car trailer so I wouldn't have to borrow his every month.

Celica Race car

Car Trailer

It was great fun; I used it for gymkhanas at first then I took it to the track where I entered in lap sprints. This was specifically for any car that was roadworthy. We would race against the clock basically trying to improve our times, we did need to have a basic speed license and be a member of an affiliated car club to cover insurance.

Another toy I had while here was a Polaris Predator 500, a quad bike or ATV (All-Terrain Vehicle), this was a sight unseen purchase that came from either Sydney or Melbourne, I can't remember which, it was ready to go as a competitive vehicle.

The first time I rode it was at the NT Titles at a track not far from Darwin.

Having no previous experience, other than riding one of the RAAF's 250cc quads around a field months earlier, this sure was going to be interesting.

The track I was to compete on was probably 3 km's long snaking in and out of the jungle with jumps, whoops and tabletops; I had never confronted anything like this before only watched on TV.

Everyone was combating the 33° heat and I think 4 or 5 laps for possibly 3 races each day, over a 2 day meet; needless to say it was gruelling.

I didn't do so well as far as race position goes, but I did complete the competition, chalking it all up as experience.

I competed in a flat track race a while later, but due to the more aggressive nature of the track, with many more turns I found it hard to get grip, and was left for dead at the back of the pack.

From what I learned when talking to other riders, they were replacing their rear tires nearly every other race meet, this was something I wasn't prepared to do.

The same tires were on the quad from the day I received it, and who knows how old they were then, although I thought they looked to be in reasonable condition.

The quad and me

Meanwhile I was moved to SPV (Special Purpose Vehicles), here we would be heavily involved in servicing and maintenance of the specific equipment used on the airfield.

Due to major exercise's being operated out of Darwin, we would carry out practice aircraft arrests prior to any jet aircraft arriving for such exercises. These would be done both in daylight and in the dark of night, where light sticks were used for signalling.

We had to get this down to a fine art, as more than one jet may be in the need to take the cable at any one time; therefore readying the system in between arrests was to be carried out post haste, as a mistake could render the cable useless.

Night arrests were especially exciting to watch; when the cable was taken and dragged along the airstrip, it would emit a shower of sparks giving a mini light show, then after the aircraft had stopped and the cable was unhooked we would work like a pack of bees, to reconfigure it in case it was needed again in a hurry.

Jet taking cable on dusk (possibly an F15)

During such an exercise, live firing was carried out by the jets involved being Australian and American fighters, FA18, F15 and the like.

This was facilitated by targets that were towed behind Lear jets; the targets were connected to cables that would be wound out from the tow aircraft once it was at the appropriate coordinates.

The Lear jets would be allocated air space over the sea, way off the coast and fly in a large circular pattern, where the fighter jets would fire on the targets with their mini guns.

I was lucky enough to be invited to go up with one of the Lear jets, we couldn't see a great deal as the target was I guess, 1 or 2 kilometres away, but every now and then off in the distance a jet could be seen coming in for the kill and the sound of the mini guns could be heard, what a rush.

Back at SPV, processing paper work and inputting data took up a lot of time and one of my main jobs when not on the runway, the same as it was in FEMS, which was ok, the only problem being the temperature in the office.

There were 2 or 3 air conditioning units in the room, due to the space that needed cooling and the number of personnel working in there, I found it so cold that every now and then I would go into the workshop to warm up.

As often as I could I would find myself a job that wasn't paperwork, whether it be a service or a breakdown to keep the boredom of the office at a minimum.

As well as the new buildings at FEMS a new building was under construction at the site of the main GEMS facility, where SPV was located, this was to replace the WWII tin building that was the main workshop. From memory the new building was a cement prefabricated structure, and was going to be smaller than the old building possibly making work space a future problem.

Despite the "input" our guys had been asked to supply, regarding what we required at the new building, very few suggestions were implemented making it seem a mere token gesture.

When new trainees finished their trade training at RAAF Wagga Wagga, they would be sent to a base to complete their on the job training.

They were also offered training that would make their job more interesting, this was offered at Darwin and I assume at other bases. This training would cover skills such as; advanced welding, lathe and mill operation, this was not compulsory, it was only for their benefit, but surprisingly some would say that it wasn't in their job description, and that they weren't interested.

Both I and the other Corporal who worked alongside me, were astonished by this attitude, both of us relished in using these skills and the ongoing thirst for knowledge in this field, we would look at each other in disbelief and would say "What", especially when we had a relatively up-to-date machine shop at our disposal.

It was evident by the mindset of some of the trainees coming through at the time, that the willingness to learn more than the prescribed minimum, had changed from years gone by, where these opportunities would have been jumped on.

In 2010, 321ECSS integrated with 13SQN, this being a reserve squadron at RAAF Darwin for many years, (having provenance from WWII and being in the direct firing line during the Japanese bombing of Darwin in 1942) whereby 321ECSS was disbanded.

The integration with reserve units was occurring at bases across Australia, enabling all the ability to share the same resources as one another, therefore giving the reserve squadrons the recognition they deserved.

13SQN patch

Every day there is what is known as "sick parade", this was for personnel who feel unwell or have hurt themselves prior to the start of work; this is carried out at the Medical Section around 0730.

One morning I attended said "sick parade" with back pain that had started in the middle of the night.

This happened as I changed position in bed. I was woken with a pain I can only describe as something like a red hot poker being driven into my lower back or lumbar that lasted for 5 – 10 minutes, so intense that I was crying out in pain.

This prompted X-rays of the area and the result was Spondylosis of the lower back or degenerative disc's, a condition thought to be exacerbated by the work practices of my job over the years.

Approximately 18 months previously, I was also diagnosed with Spondylosis of the cervical spine or neck, causing a lump to be evident at the back of my neck, I had physio therapy treatment to help the situation, and the same was to be done for my lower back.

Some of the physio methods were questionable though, I was told I didn't have a curve in my spine, that it was more or less straight.

The physio gave me an exercise to manipulate my spine, supposedly creating a curve. This entailed rolling up a towel and lying on it where it was running up my spine, applying pressure to somehow or other create a curve, not having heard of anything like this before, I decided to give it a go anyway, but it didn't seem to do anything other than create more pain.

When discussing these problems with my GP, I suggested the possibility of a medical discharge and would that be appropriate at this time.

I had already looked into this to know where I stood and she agreed, acknowledging that a medical discharge would indeed help the situation.

These conditions as well as the arthritis in my knees, along with what was referred to as, bilateral wrists, weren't going to get any better and if I continued doing the same work they would progressively worsen.

I wondered why this wasn't suggested to me rather than by me earlier, and I still don't know, but I have read that many servicemen see the Defence Force as their family, and when medically discharged some haven't handled it too well, therefore doctors are hesitant in suggesting it at times, that may have been a possibility, I will never know.

Going in a more or less familiar direction to what I was in years past, an Orthopaedic specialist was organised to carry out a whole of body assessment which included; my full range of movement, weight carrying capabilities, grip strength etc. When the report was received by my GP, she restricted my work load to office duties only, conveniently the position of Officer in charge of

MCS (Maintenance Control Section) had become vacant, due to the Defence Civilian in that role was going on maternity leave, opening it for me.

A medical discharge involves a panel of doctors and high ranking officers specialising in this kind of procedure. All the facts are looked at very closely, as well as any other positions available in my trade where I could be employed, with restrictions of this nature; the process took around 12 months.

In the mean time I was in charge of MCS, a mind numbing job where 95% of the time I was sitting there twiddling my thumbs, I don't know what the civilian normally in this position did all day.

Time marched on and eventually the decision was finally handed down, and I was to be medically discharged on the 18 DEC, 2011, this time I was unable to reenlist or join the reserves indefinitely.

Over the next few months I organised my final clearances, and handed everything back in that needed to be, believe it or not this included items such as socks, long johns, towels and boots.

My send-off gave me an opportunity to say a few words and I was presented with a plaque as is normal.

As part of my speech I said I didn't particularly enjoy my posting at Darwin, this I regret saying as I didn't clarifying why.

This was due to the humidity being so stifling this time around, 3 years without a dry season to speak of, enough to drive a person crazy.

When I said this, I noticed some disgruntled looks, but it didn't register till later, I think some may have taken it personally, and then it was too late, sorry guys.

A few stayed on after my presentation to have a drink with me, and asked what I meant when I said I wasn't too happy with Darwin, they understood my reasoning's.

This was a big turning point for me, knowing I had to leave this life style permanently. Working for the RAAF was the best three decisions I had made in my working life, it still is part of my life, I find myself thinking back on it to some extent every day.

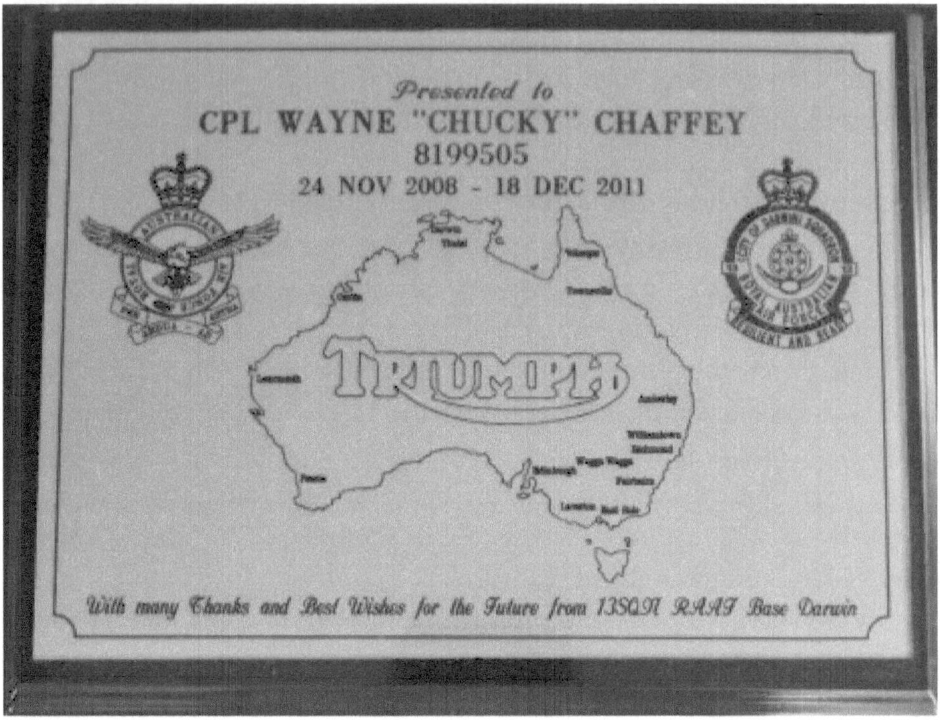

My final "Presento"

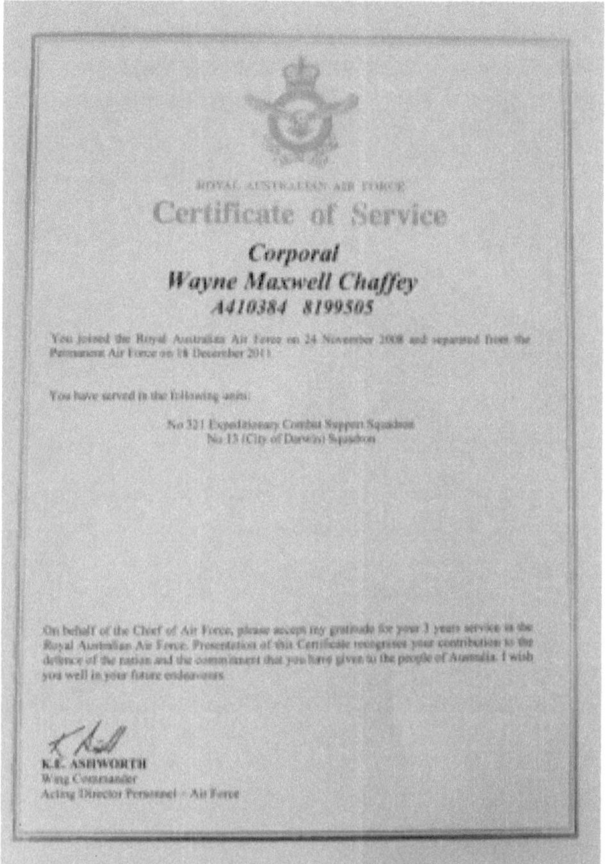

Final Certificate of Service

Adelaide was to be my discharge destination; this is where my daughters and their families where living at the time.

The Ghan, a tourism passenger train that travels between Adelaide and Darwin, was the way I travelled down with my car in a carriage at the rear.

The train stopped off at Alice Springs approximately half way, for a short break, with the journey taking 54 hours all up.

Gold class was the way to go, where I had a private cabin along with silver service dinning, I figured I won't be doing this again so let's do it right.

The Ghan

Stop off at Alice Springs

As a finishing note I would like to recap on why I kept coming back.

The most important reason being the security associated with the Defence Force on a whole, once you were in, it was basically for life if you wanted it that way.

Obviously not in my case as the curiosity of what may lay around the corner was always in my mind, and having the knowledge of what working in civilian life was like, also beckoned me to have a look at what was happening there.

Other reasons included: the comradeship and teamwork associated with fellow workers. Due to the nature of the specialised equipment we worked with, there was at times, the need for complex fault finding, where one would have to call on other members with more experience, to help solve problems and most were happy to help.

The emphasis was always on safety first and regardless of the time involved in making a situation safe, one would feel confident that it was.

There would always be someone there to cover your back if needed, regardless of it being a work or personal problem and this could range from the guy working next to you up to your CO.

Oh and did I mention the food, just in case I didn't. I would eat lunch at the mess for a majority of the time I was enlisted, the choices would be from one of 3 different roasts e.g. turkey, pork, lamb or from 4 or 5 main courses. Then a selection of roast and boiled vegies, different breads and normally a soup of the day as well as a salad bar.

This was followed up by a selection of made on the premises and bought in deserts.

The RAAF, without a doubt, had the best selection out of the 3 services and I think the cost was around $5.00 in 2011.

I'm reasonably happy with the way I handled my career, even though I lost seniority each time I re-joined, but when I did reenlist, it was like coming home again after a long break.

Before I go I would like to touch on what life was like once I arrived in Adelaide.

Just before I left Darwin I found a house I liked on line, and asked my daughter to look through it, she was impressed and told me it was just as the pictures depicted, I put an offer on it, and it was accepted.

The house was not far from my daughters, in a suburb called Surrey Downs, a pleasant area where I was lucky enough to have some good neighbours that were happy to have a chat from time to time.

To alleviate the feeling of being on my own I bought myself a companion dog.

This one being an ex-show girl (boxer) that needed to be rehomed, due to new dogs coming through and not enough room for old ones.

The Department of Veterans Affairs (DVA) put me through some rehabilitation courses to see if there was anything I would like to do, this included work related and self-development courses, and the only thing that interested me was a photographic course, through this I gained a diploma of basic photography.

Now I'm happily retired doing my own thing i.e. rebuilding damaged motorcycles, making things on my 3d printer and cnc router, maintaining my car and house and doing things for my wife Huey Yi.

Thanks for taking the time to read about my experiences during my Air Force career.

I loved what I did and would do it all again if I had the chance, albeit with some fine tuning.

All the best

Chuck.

Legend

RAAF Royal Australian Air Force

1RTU No1 Recruit Training Unit

3AD No3 Aircraft Depot

AWR Air Weapons Range

JLUN Joint Logistic Unit North

AAS Aircraft Arresting System

GEMS Ground Equipment Maintenance Section

FEMS Fuel Equipment Maintenance Section

SPV Special Purpose Vehicles

MCS Maintenance Control Section

CO Commanding Officer

ACR Aircraftsman Recruit

AC Aircraftsman

LAC Leading Aircraftsman

CPL Corporal

SGT Sergeant

FSGT Flight Sergeant

WOFF Warrant Officer

PTI Physical Training Instructor

MTFITT Motor Transport Fitter

GSEFITT Ground Support Equipment Fitter

About the Publisher

Established in 2024
Published in South Australia